A Beautiful STORM

Finding our Purpose on our ALS Journey

ALISHA BYRD-CLARK
& ALEX CLARK

Copyright © 2022 Alisha Byrd-Clark & Alex Clark.

All rights reserved. No part of this book may be reproduced, stored, or transmitted by any means—whether auditory, graphic, mechanical, or electronic—without written permission of both publisher and author, except in the case of brief excerpts used in critical articles and reviews. Unauthorized reproduction of any part of this work is illegal and is punishable by law.

ISBN: 979-8-88640-349-7 (sc)
ISBN: 979-8-88640-350-3 (hc)
ISBN: 979-8-88640-351-0 (e)

Because of the dynamic nature of the Internet, any web addresses or links contained in this book may have changed since publication and may no longer be valid. The views expressed in this work are solely those of the author and do not necessarily reflect the views of the publisher, and the publisher hereby disclaims any responsibility for them.

One Galleria Blvd., Suite 1900, Metairie, LA 70001
1-888-421-2397

Dedication

IN MEMORY OF

Jessie Byrd, Sr., Minnie Young Byrd, Efffie Louise Clark Thomas & Mary Louise Gibson, Gregory Gibson, Terrence Hayes, Clay Anthony Sturdivant, Larry Walker, James and Daisey Walker

BECAUSE OF YOU

To our children Devin, Rushawn and Chastity, having you as children has been our greatest joy. You have been given the Melanated GENIUS and Melanated BEAUTY blueprint to not only be great but EXTRAORDINARY. Use these tools and make us proud.

To our grandstars, our future leaders of the world Aariana and Karie and our siblings Shawn Clark, Hen Norman, Nadia Sturdivant, Yoshida Thorton, Latrice Walker-Blount, Latosha Gibson, Laquessa Forte we love you beyond words.

To our parents Patricia B, Sturdivant, Margaret Clark Robinson and Garry Robinson, we have had the most exceptional foundation and support system. Thank you for being consistent with your love and support.

To Gemstones & COMPASS Leadership Academy Always apply your COMPASS and remember EXCELLENCE is a MINDSET.

CONTENTS

Acknowledgements vii
Foreword ix
Preface xi

1. Electric Charge 1
Mistaken Identity 2
First 21 Days 4
Gemstones & COMPASS Leadership Academy 8

2. Wind 11
ALS Diagnosis 12
Stem Cell Transplant 17

3. Clear Skies 19
Proposal 20
Confessions 22
Our Wedding Day 23

4. Hurricane 27
Respiratory Failure 28
Apologies 35

5. Tides & Waves 37
Chatter 38
Our Village 40
Through It All 41
Eternally Grateful 43
Divine Connection 45
The Four Queens 50

The Hero I Know..55
King Alex: Our Healer...56
Family...58
My Brother's Keeper...61
Second Opinion 64
Celli..66
Unlikeliest of Friendships 70
A Mother's Heart 75

6. Summer Breeze 79
Sacrifices 80
Impact..83
Good Enough 85
Resiliency 86

7. Earthquake 87
When it Hurts to Live..88
Extended Stay 90
2-Year Anniversary 92
Promises...93
War...95
Transitioning..96
Living On Empty..99
Dying Empty 101
God Answered 102

8. Rainbow 105
He Lived 106
He Found His Purpose... 107

9. Melanated Genius..109
Quotes 113
Jewels of the Day.. 115
The Look in His Eyes... 120

ACKNOWLEDGEMENTS

Alex and I were beyond grateful to have had the most incredible doctors, nurses and respiratory therapists. They went above and beyond to provide the best quality of care for us. To them, Alex was more than just a patient. He was family.

We established an unbreakable bond that will continue for years to come. We have been told that nurses are not supposed to get close to their patients; however, it's very difficult not to get close to Alex as he always offered words of wisdom and encouragement when others needed it most.

He opened and shared his heart with them, and they were receptive and did the same. From the bottom of my heart, though, admittedly, it feels woefully inadequate, let me simply say a most heartfelt and humble say THANK YOU!

Doctors: Agbebi Abayomi, Lester Brown, James Carress, Leighanne Dorton, Kiran Jagarlamundi, Corwin Rankin.

Intensivists: Jamie Douthit, Andrea Eudy, Neil Patel, Zeeshan Ahmad

Home Health Nurses: Maria Epps, Keyonta Pemberton, Angela Smith, Kim Washington, Gloria Woodruff.

Team Leads/Charge Nurses: Michelle Broome, Amanda Johnson, Kristin McDaniel, Michelle Prather, Nyrstan Pruett.

Novant Medical Center Registered Nurses: Angie Allgood, Jamie Anderson, Megan Arney, Taylor Arey, Markie Childers, John Duplisea, Caitlyn Edly, Caleb Foster, Teresa Gaegan, Jennifer Goodman, Whitney Graham, Ashley Grubb, Ashley Hendricks, Justin Knight, Jackie

Ledford, Kristin Losh, Jenna Lyerly, Kristin Mahaley, Jessi Meredith, Lauren Miller, Megan Phillips, Shelley Quan, Kaylen Renfrow, Beverly Smith, Tiffany Tallent, Janine Terpstra, Amber Thomas, Meredith Triplett, Haley Wagnor, Summer Wilson.

Novant Medical Center Respiratory Therapist: Tina Burr Alexander, Kelly Bowers, Wanda Brandenburg, Carrie Callahan, Charity Buie Cape, Connie Dillard, Victoria Featherstone, Darlene Galloway, Beth Gill, Shelly Hatley, Erica Hurt, Liz Lefler, Ashley Shaver Lombard, Kathyrn Overcash Lopez, Angela Lucas, Barry Myers, Tabby Plummer, Kristen Rimmer, Candy Smith, Lisa Tadlock, Drew White, Thai Yang, Mike Young.

To Linda Brown, Tashara Sanders, Ed and Susan Norvall, Fred and Alice Stanback, David Post, Mona Lisa Wallace, Bill Graham, Matt Barr, Larry Cloninger, Steve Fisher, Paul and Sue Fisher, Lee Wallace, Gerry Wood, Mikey Wetzel, Greg Shields, Victor Wallace: What is understood does not have to be said. Just know that you made a difference in Alex's battle with ALS and for that—as well as for each of you—I will always be grateful.

FOREWORD

A circle is endless. It has no beginning or end, which means it goes on forever and symbolizes infinity—just as the wedding ring symbolizes never-ending love and commitment without boundaries.

It signifies eternal love, just as it should be. Soulmates, or as they call themselves "Sympathetic Souls," are partners for life, as well as partners in life. They're not your competition but instead bring completion.

As you read this beautiful love story, please understand that time is precious and none of us knows how much time we truly have. Realize that time and timing are everything. Alex and Alisha made the best of the time GOD gave them together, and they lived life to the fullest. Their story is a captivating, true tale of love that will ignite a fire inside you and make you realize how important it is to value each precious moment you have. Moreover, their story will make you, value the ones with whom you're blessed to share your time and space with. Most of all, Alex's and Alisha's story will make you want to love passionately and relentlessly because you truly don't know how much time you have left on this journey called life.

Alex and Alisha never claimed to be perfect, but as you read their story, you will realize they were perfect for each other. They became fully aware of their purpose as one and set out to pursue it. They realized life is too short for bickering and warring against one another. They decided to walk the path that GOD laid out for their lives, and in doing so they came together and made magic out of imperfection. They collided, and what manifested was... A Beautiful Storm.

Tara D. White

PREFACE

As newlyweds, you look forward to your honeymoon. You also make plans as husband and wife. Our plans were simultaneously simple and lofty: expand our business, build our first home and travel the world.

Sadly, Alex and I didn't get to build a house together. And instead of traveling the world, we made repeated trips to the hospital. As we were getting adjusted to being a married couple and learning more about one another, we were also learning the in's and out of the healthcare system and getting to know people who would provide exceptional care for Alex.

When I think back to our wedding day and the vows we made before God, our family and friends, I smile warmly as I remember our covenant—that regardless of any challenges we faced, we would face them as one.

During our marriage, every vow we made was tested—particularly in sickness and in health. We hadn't even opened all our wedding gifts—much less sent thank you cards to our wedding guests—when sickness came knocking at our door.

Just a year after Alex and I said, "I Do," a lot had changed in our lives. Our vow to love and cherish each other kept us going. Our love for each other grew stronger, creating a tie that was neither breakable nor measurable. Our love was divinely blessed. There was never a doubt that we were each other's destiny.

In my India Arie voice, "He's givin' me love, so steady. He touches my heart, now I'm ready. He touches my soul and my spirit. He's givin' me love so steady." In other words, Alex never missed a beat, not when it came to loving me, praying over me, encouraging me, inspiring me or being sympathetic to my soul's every need. He was my handsome, intelligent, wise and wonderful husband. He was a great father to our children and a provider and mentor to many other children—always imparting a voice of hope and revelation that inspired those who had the privilege of being in his company.

I have plenty of dates to remember, but July 11, 2014, is a date I will never forget! On our ALS journey, we CELEBRATED LIFE daily. We LOVED hard. We valued our FAMILY. We found PEACE. We relied on our FAITH, and we experienced HAPPINESS daily... #GODIS

1

Electric Charge

MISTAKEN IDENTITY

My mother, daughter and I attended an interdenominational citywide revival at a local church. Afterwards, I saw a familiar face and decided to speak, only to receive a rather weird and cold look as he said, "peace and blessings." Come again, I thought! I must admit, I was in my feelings because I thought Harvey was acting brand new. Ladies, you know how it is when you speak to a man you know, and he acts funny. Kind of rubs you the wrong way. Well, when I tell you I was bothered by this, I most definitely was because "Harvey" and I were cooler than a fan. I turned to my mom and daughter and told them that Harvey was tripping, acting as though he's too good to speak.

About a week later, I was having a conversation with a family member and mutual friend who mentioned Alex, aka Duke. Unfortunately, I didn't know who he was at the time.

Years ago, I'd heard about Duke but never had the pleasure of meeting him. As the conversation continued, our mutual friend brought up the church situation and, according to Alex—who I had mistakenly thought was Harvey—not only did I run up on him in church. He thought my name was Tasha. The nerve of some men! Our mutual friend later mentioned that Alex had been inquiring about me. Go figure! So, now he wants to know about this so-called crazy lady named Tasha who, to hear him tell it, ran up on him in church. Following me? We both thought the other was someone else.

On my birthday, one of my cousins told me that she'd seen Alex at a party and, yet again, he'd asked about me, the so-called crazy lady he thought was named Tasha. Alex ended up sending me a DM as the youth call it. (That's a direct message in case you didn't know.) In the message, he asked about the protocol of my nonprofit organization.

For me to have been "the crazy lady," he sure was being nosey all over my social media pages. His message to me proved he was just as crazy as I supposedly was.

It just so happens I have some receipts to tell the story! According to my Facebook Messenger, on May 30, 2014, his words to me were, "Peace and Blessings...Didn't I see you last Friday at Jerusalem Church? If I'm correct, you asked me if I remembered you." *Incorrect boo*, I thought to myself. *I spoke and you looked confused.*

Since I missed the message and didn't respond—I should remind you I didn't know who Alex was at this point—Mr. Persistent decided to send another message via Facebook Messenger on June 5, 2014. "Peace and Blessings... I saw a mutual friend of ours and he told me that you thought I was Harvey. People think he's my little brother; however, my name is Alex. No hurt, no harm. If you don't mind me asking, what is the protocol of your organization? Peace." *Still wanting to know more about this so-called "crazy lady, huh?"* I thought.

Mr. Persistent sent a third message on July 10, 2014. "Peace and Blessings, Queen... I was told that you were talking about me. If you have something to say here's my number. Peace, King." Ok, so now suddenly he's addressing me, the so-called "crazy lady," as "Queen." Was Mr. Persistent getting fresh with me?

I finally responded to Alex via Facebook Messenger and later decided to call him. I must admit, the phone call was well worth it...

FIRST 21 DAYS

After a series of messages, both directly to each other and through friends, Alex and I finally met face-to-face on July 11, 2014. We discussed business matters, and during our time together he shared with me the first four chapters of the book he'd soon release, "The Four Queens: Understanding the Powers of Your Crown." I found myself begging him to let me co-author the book, but he shot me down numerous times.

His book was simply amazing in my opinion. It was profoundly, eloquently and tastefully written, painting a vivid depiction of the attributes, morals and downfalls of women. I was amazed at how he took the four queens from a simple deck of playing cards and transformed them into complete queens that women should strive to become. He kept my attention from beginning to the end by carefully weaving and blending textures and fibers to create an amazing queen who's loving, ambitious, savvy, disciplined and graceful.

In fact, "The Four Queens" inspired me to do a reassessment of the desires of my heart, to become more in tune with my spirit, to live life to the fullest and to become a better me. Because of "The Four Queens," I began to understand the POWERS of my crown while becoming well-suited for any given day. Despite not allowing me to co-author with him, Alex trusted me enough to assist with some very important parts of the book process.

A few days later, which I remember as if it were yesterday, Alex asked me to meet him at the park. When I arrived, he was removing a blanket and lawn chair from the trunk. We greeted one another with a smile and hug and found a spot underneath a tree.

While I was placing the blanket on the ground, I turned around to find Alex taking off his shirt and pants. *Really, dude? You feel this comfortable around me already*? I didn't just think it. I said it. His response was it was hot, and he was still wearing some clothes. As I shook my head, he chuckled and shared the most beautiful smile, which ignited something within me and touched my soul.

As time passed, Alex asked for twenty-one days to change my life. So here I am thinking what will this man do or say during these twenty-one days? I was curious and the request was questionable, but with his smile and the sincerity of his words and actions, I couldn't help but grant it.

I reached out to another mutual friend of ours, Babalawo Bakojo Oguntola, for a more in-depth interpretation of the significance of the number twenty-one. His interpretation was twenty-one is one of the most powerful numbers in the spiritual realm. When added, two plus one equals three, and the number three means completion.

These numbers were a representation of the fullness of who Alex was, who I am and what we were going to make together, Babalawo told me. Our own entity. For twenty-one days, he chose you and you chose him. In addition, he said, the number twenty-one is the Phenomenon of Choice, meaning we have the power to choose. For the two of us to become who he (the head) wanted, we would have to both lose a little bit of ourselves.

You must know by now that my curiosity remained at an all-time high and our conversations gave me more insight regarding the depth and complexity of his mind—all of which kept me wanting to know more and more about him.

So, for twenty-one days we had a "parking lot" friendship if you will. We met at Cookout, Walmart, Kmart, the library—you name it. We also met at random places.

During one parking lot outing, we found ourselves discussing The Five Love Languages. I asked him to humor me and rank his Five Love Languages in order according to his wants, desires and beliefs. Remember, The Five Love Languages are Words of Affirmation, Acts of Service, Receiving Gifts, Quality Time and Physical Touch. I told him I considered quality time most important because of previous relationships in which quality time was what I most desired but least received.

Shortly after sharing, I asked for his order and he told me that you can't have one without the others as they're all equally important. I gave him a look that conveyed I understood what he was saying but still felt that one must be more important than the others. He held his stance that they were equally important, even expounding that they are intricate pieces of a whole and we never know which one we'll need to use at any given moment. By polarizing them, he said, we don't take advantage of each one. They may be labeled love languages, he continued, but in reality, they're principles that are the crux of every successful relationship.

Ladies, I don't have to tell you that by now I was starting to dig this man's mind, the way he thought and the way he expressed himself. So, for the next couple of days, we continued meeting in different locations. I felt myself being drawn to this man who was examining the deepest parts of my soul without it feeling invasive. By day ten, we were completing each other's sentences. Of course it started freaking me out a little bit, started feeling "too good to be true," so I started questioning God, asking Him who in the world was this man and how were we able to build such a solid foundation for our friendship in a mere twenty-one days.

For once in my life, I was finally being sought after by the man God created just for me. He was oh so very handsome, the most intelligent man I had ever met. He was loving and had a heart of gold. He met all of the requirements that were included on my list of qualities, which I had hidden in my bible. In other words, ladies, he checked all of the boxes. (Smile.)

The way he looked at me, not to mention the way he respected and treated his mother and me, said a lot about Alex. He courted me and was never in a hurry for anything. Instead, he took his time getting to know the complete me. Although he couldn't care less about and wasn't the least bit threatened by my previous relationships, he inquired about them enough to ensure he didn't make the same mistakes those men made, which caused them to lose me.

Needless to say, after those twenty-one calendar days came and went, Alex and I continued having in-depth conversations about life, family, relationships and community—all of which were equally important to our hearts.

GEMSTONES & COMPASS LEADERSHIP ACADEMY

After several more indepth conversations, our focus shifted and we started laying the foundation for our non-profit organizations, Gemstones and COMPASS Leadership Academy. We worked on our plan, which was filled with ideas and desires that were shared by the youth in our community. A few months later, we were having our grand opening for youth.

We were putting our plan into motion. We decided to be the change we wanted to see, starting with our youth, the future leaders of the world. On our opening day, we had twenty kids whose parents enrolled them in a program with the potential to change their lives. We opened with prayer by my Aunt Katie because we wanted God to be included and at the forefront of everything we were striving to accomplish.

After explaining our mission and "why" to our extended family, we charged the parents, who were attentively listening, to allow and trust us to do our job without undoing what we taught to their children. The good thing is they trusted us, appreciated the program we put in motion and supported us throughout our journey.

Every month, we allowed our youth to come up with creative ideas and encouraged them to think outside the box when it came to being the best version of themselves and giving back to our community. We wanted them to be part of the change and become vested in something greater than them.

We taught them the importance of our core values, leadership, integrity, responsibility and scholarship. We instilled in them the importance of never blending in because they were born to stand out because they were not ordinary but instead EXTRAORDINARY.

Our expectations for them were set extremely high, and to wear a shirt with our logo on it, they had to be the best representation of us and what we stood for. We taught them why they were TRENDSETTERS and why EXCELLENCE was a mindset.

Before long, those same youths who were shy, very timid and considered introverts were ready to conquer the world.

Alex was an amazing chess player and used the game to apply life lessons to our youth. Our meetings revolved around conversations about choices, consequences and the ripple effects of positive and negative decisions.

He introduced them to Johari Window, a technique that helps people better understand their relationship with themselves and others. Basically, it examines how the who, what, when, where and why play a major role in the unknown things they cannot see, or their blind spots if you will. It looks at things people see to which they're oblivious. It also dissects their potential, areas they haven't begun to tap into, and their secrets.

Our youth were introduced to things that will never be found in textbooks and were exposed to real, hardcore life lessons—Alex Clark lessons and chess lessons. It was all designed to remind them that every move they make in life matters.

One of the major goals Alex and I set for our organization was providing college scholarships for our high school graduates. We worked hard, used our own money in the beginning and invested in youth who have the potential to be great. Fortunately, we exceeded our projected goals and saw the seeds we planted blossom and flourish into young adults who will no doubt become productive men and women.

One of our greatest joys has been investing into someone else's life and seeing an excellent ROI (return on investment) when the young person does well and carries himself or herself in an upstanding manner.

We became vested in our community by devising creative measures without reinventing the wheel. In short, we presented fresh ideas to our community and SOARED!

We wanted to set the best example for our own children as well as those in our program. Our hard work and community involvement led to awards and accolades we never imagined receiving. We tried to constantly demonstrate Luke 12:48, "To whom much is given, much is required." We took seriously the responsibility of managing the businesses with which God had blessed us. And we took even more seriously the responsibility of nurturing and instructing children whose parents had placed them in our care. Alex and I found every way imaginable to give back to our community, and we were blessed to have been chosen as recipients of numerous awards and notable recognitions. We were very surprised and appreciative to receive the Key to the City by Salisbury's first African American Mayor, Al Heggins, who designated January 3rd as Alex and Alisha Day. The recognitions made us work harder and more diligently to bring about change in our community.

2

Wind

ALS DIAGNOSIS

Everyday Alex and I took walks around the neighborhood. We worked out during the day and walked downtown in the evenings. I remember it like it was yesterday... One evening we were getting prepared for a walk and he started limping. I asked what was going on with his leg, whether he had possibly sprained his ankle. He said he wasn't sure but was going to make a doctor's appointment to get it checked out.

The next thing I knew; we were going to different specialists to determine what was wrong. We were told by one doctor that it might be a Vitamin D deficiency, so he started taking Vitamin D to see if that would abate the problem.

After seeing no progress, we were on to an acupuncture specialist to see if that would clear up the problem. It didn't.

Then Alex was sent to a neurologist for additional testing. Although that doctor wasn't one hundred percent certain, he thought Alex's problem was ALS, or Amyotrophic Lateral Sclerosis. It's also known as Lou Gehrig's Disease, named after the New York Yankees baseball player who was stricken with it in 1939. ALS is a progressive, neurodegenerative disease that affects nerve cells in the brain and spinal cord. With ALS, the brain loses connection with the muscles, causing people to lose their ability to walk, eat, talk and eventually breath. Although there are several forms of ALS, unfortunately there are no cures for any of them.

Both Alex and I were hardcore researchers, so we started conducting our own research about ALS. We wondered how in the world did he, out of all people, get ALS. Although there are genetic ties, no one in his family had it.

Just like with anyone who has been told he or she has a condition of any sort, Alex wanted a second opinion. And so did I. So we flew to Chicago, stayed with some relatives for two weeks and went to a specialist at the University of Chicago.

We wanted to be certain simply because ALS and MS mirror each other. I didn't want Alex to have either one of those illnesses, but between the two if he had to have one, I certainly was praying for the diagnosis to be MS versus ALS. Unfortunately, the specialist at the University of Chicago confirmed the ALS diagnosis. So, what next? We didn't know anyone who had this disease to talk to regarding what to expect. I remember Alex turning to me and asking, "What are you going to do?" My response to him was, "I'm going to be here for you regardless. I'm not going anywhere." So here we are back at square one trying to figure out our next move.

We asked questions. We researched everything. We joined the ALS Association and support groups.

Alex was a vegetarian for eighteen years, but after learning that his ALS onset could have been caused by a lack of protein, we changed our eating habits and slowly added meat to his diet. I promised to give up red meat, pork and everything else I loved if he agreed to eat fish, turkey and chicken. This nutrition adjustment wasn't easy for him, but he was willing to acquiesce because his life was on the line.

People in our community noticed the difference in his walk and hands but never felt comfortable asking what was going on because they knew Alex was a very private person.

While sitting at a traffic light one afternoon, I decided to go on Facebook. The first thing I saw was a post from Alex disclosing his ALS diagnosis. I pulled over and cried because Alex, this very private person, had decided to let the world into his life. He decided to put his pride aside because this was going to be the most difficult, challenging journey of his life. On August 21, 2017, his post read:

Facebook Family...

PRIDE has always been one of my greatest adversaries, but today, we're going to WAR! because what I share with you can possibly assist someone else.

With that being said, two years ago I was diagnosed with Amyotrophic Lateral Sclerosis, commonly known as ALS or Lou Gehrig's Disease. I've had every test that you can think of from Baptist Hospital's top neurologist. I even flew to Chicago to get a second opinion. NOTHING CHANGED as far as the diagnosis is concerned. However, he suggested that I do some research on Stem Cell Treatment. About ALS, it's a neurodegenerative disease that causes muscle atrophy, respiratory disorders, cognitive impairment, trouble speaking and can lead to paralysis or an early death. I know some of you that I work with in the community have probably taken note of how I walk now compared to then. To maintain the integrity of our relationship, the progression of ALS is the reason. It's easy to question the Creator and ask why me? And for the record, I don't look at what I'm dealing with as some kind of punishment because WE all have things we must endure and overcome. See, however, I've accepted my body is going through some serious changes, embraced the challenge, and I'M GONNA SHOW YOU WHAT FAITH LOOKS LIKE IN ACTION. So, when you hear me say I'm giving my LIFE to assist our youth with avoiding going down the wrong path, I mean that literally.

At this point, my only option is Stem Cell Treatment, and I will be hosting an ALS AWARENESS FUNDRAISER, which includes dinner and entertainment, for $50.00

on September 9th at Livingstone College's Hospitality Center to work towards my teams' goal of raising $50,000.00. If you know any resources that may be available, PLEASE SHARE them with me. I must admit that was a real challenge, but my team insisted I share what I'm dealing with to bring awareness to this deadly disease known as ALS. Sorry it took so long. Now will you FIGHT WITH ME? I started a group page called #HelpAlexBeatALS where you can find more information. Thanks.

Alex had overcome some major obstacles in his life, but nothing and I mean nothing was as complex or could compare to this.

To hear his cry for family and community support simultaneously made me proud of him while affixing a huge knot in my stomach. When I asked him how he really felt about being diagnosed with ALS, he said:

"Being diagnosed with ALS was at first unbelievable, and it took some time to fully wrap my mind around what I had just been told. When I first got a conclusive diagnosis, it was surreal because I never thought I would be diagnosed with a terminal illness that others say is incurable. At that moment, it was like I was tone deaf because I just couldn't believe what I just heard. After listening to all of the speculation and after enduring all of the tests, to hear someone tell me this, that ALS is what most resembles what's wrong with me, was indescribable.

My mind was racing. I was trying to wrap my mind around what I had just been told. Being told in so many words that you have a limited amount of time left, without the person actually saying those words, was disheartening to say the least. Having my mom and dad and my then-girlfriend, now wife in the room at the time was comforting, but it was still hard for me to digest mentally.

Of course why me and how did this happen to me questions were running through my mind. I felt angry. I immediately wanted another opinion because this just couldn't be happening to me of all people. Although we all heard the same diagnosis, it seems like you could hear a pin drop in the room. Seeing the looks of disbelief on the faces in the room made me dig deep into my spirit to stay strong in that moment.

In my mind, I was thinking, out of all the diseases in the world, how did I get diagnosed with the one that has no known cure."

STEM CELL TRANSPLANT

A few days after Alex came forth about his diagnosis, our families got together and put a plan in motion. Stem Cell Transplants are very expensive and can be painful. We were told this new, alternative medicine was designed to potentially bring symptom relief, slow, halt or even reverse the condition progression.

At this point, we were optimistic and very hopeful for a positive outcome. Several fundraisers were held to assist Alex with getting the necessary funds for his Stem Cell Treatment.

We researched numerous reputable companies, found what we were looking for and headed to Delray Beach, Florida.

On the first day there, Alex had to take one ninety-minute dive in a hyperbaric oxygen chamber to start the stimulation of the stem cells. The day before his treatment, he took three ninety-minute dives.

On the morning of his procedure, we meditated and prayed for God to cover us and the doctors who would provide care. We also had another consultation with the doctor about what to expect before, during and after the procedure.

Since ALS causes muscle deterioration, Alex had begun to lose weight a year after his diagnosis. His loss of body fat caused the doctor to have a rough time trying to determine the right spot to inject the stem cells in his spine. During the procedure, Alex became overwhelmed, his blood pressure dropped and he began to feel faint. We had to give him a few minutes to readjust before continuing.

Alex stem cell transplant was successful without any adverse reactions. We went back to the hotel so that he could rest before our flight the next day. Our prayer before bed was Lord, it's in your hands.

3

Clear Skies

PROPOSAL

My grandfather, Jesse Byrd Sr., was very instrumental in my upbringing, as he and my grandmother, Minnie Byrd, raised me from age seven to adulthood. Not only did he tell me how a man is supposed to love, care for and treat a woman, he demonstrated it for 74 years in his marriage to my grandmother. Once Alex became *extra sweet* on me, I decided to introduce him to my grandparents. Immediately, there was a solid connection between him and my grandfather.

Introducing my grandparents to a guy was so unheard of because I was very particular about who I brought into their home. So they knew out the gate that Alex had to be someone special. The three of them talked and talked and talked about life, growing up and other things. Once they got to a stopping point, my Minnie Min turned to Alex only to ask, "What are you waiting for?" Alex looked confused at first but later caught on to what she meant. She knew within her heart that Alex was the one for me.

Several months later, we visited my grandparents and this time, Alex asked my grandfather for my hand in marriage. With a huge smile on my grandfather's face, he quickly said "yes, you can marry her". My grandmother who was overprotective in her own right said "you didn't ask me", as she smiled while offering her care bear hug.

One Friday night after dinner, Alex and I decided to take the long way home. Since we were unable to take a stroll downtown because of his inability to walk long distances, we rode around instead. As it started to rain, he asked me to drive down Long Street, which leads from Salisbury to East Spencer.

When we arrived at the end of the street, he asked me to pull into the church parking lot. Now, this is the same church where I mistakenly thought he was Harvey and he mistakenly thought I was Tasha. I pulled in, and he mentioned how our roots and foundation started here and how funny it was that we both thought the other was someone else. He went on to say that the downpour accurately summarized where we were in our relationship at this point. Specifically, Alex turned to me and said, "Queen, our relationship has been a Beautiful Storm."

He began to thank me for being there and for not turning my back on him after he was diagnosed with ALS. Then he reached into his jacket pocket and pulled out a black box. As he opened it, he said, "I asked your grandfather for permission and you are the only one I want on the remainder of this journey with me. Will you marry me?" My only response—besides yes, of course—was "What took you so long?"

I was most definitely on the proverbial cloud nine. To be the future Mrs. Alex Clark had me smiling and beaming with excitement. When we arrived at home, we took several pictures so we could announce our engagement publicly on social media. Let me tell you, our family and friends went crazy simply because we had done an excellent job of keeping our personal life private. They knew we were business partners but not that we were involved. Now it was official. Alex had asked me to be his wife and I had said yes. God heard my prayers. God kept his promise to me. Now, I had a wedding to plan.

CONFESSIONS

My grandfather once promised me that he'd live long enough to see me get married; however, years after stating that he began having health issues. Being in and out of the hospital on a regular basis almost became his new normal. In fact, there were several times when he and Alex would be in the hospital not only at the same time, but on the same floor just a few doors from each other. I had to stress to them the importance of not having to compete for my love.

During one of Alex's hospital stays, we had an indepth conversation about our future and how important it was for me to get married while my grandparents were still living.

I told him that my grandfather had made a promise to me that he would live long enough to see me get married. One more serious hospital stay quickened our steps to the altar. We had already set our wedding date and had made several plans. Yet one Sunday morning out of the blue, Alex asked me if I was ready to get married. "Of course I am," I responded. However, I didn't realize then that he was talking about the next week. He mentioned my grandfather's health and the fact that he wanted me to be able to legally help him make more sound decisions regarding his health. Alex said to me, "I will make sure you have the wedding of your dreams on the date we chose, but I don't want to prolong this any longer."

So Alex and I, my grandparents and a few of our close family and friends assembled at my grandparents' home on February 4, 2018, for a private ceremony in their living room. To be able to have them witness not only this milestone but my happiness is something I will cherish forever.

OUR WEDDING DAY

From This Moment On

From this moment, life has begun
From this moment, you are the one
Right beside you are where I belong
From this moment on
From this moment, I have been blessed
I live only for your happiness
And for your love, I'd give my last breath
From this moment on
I give my hand to you with all my heart
I can't wait to live my life with you; I can't wait to start
You and I will never be apart
My dreams came true because of you
From this moment as long as I live
I will love you; I promise you this
There is nothing I wouldn't give
From this moment on...

Shania Twain

So there we were in a room filled with three hundred fifty guests. The time had come for us to share and profess our love before those closest to our hearts. The venue was beautifully decorated, and our thirty-five-member bridal party was stunning.

My grandfather wasn't feeling well and was unable to give me away, but it just so happened I had my grandmother "Minnie Min" on standby.

As the music began playing, I felt a huge knot in my stomach. Although Alex and I were already married and held onto our "little kept secret," I was still nervous. My baby sister sang "The One He Kept For Me" by Maurette Brown Clark (no relation to Alex.) The song's words resonated deep within my soul because Alex *was* the one God not only delayed for me but also the one I dreamed about and prayed for. He was my love's desire.

Alex sat in his wheelchair because walking and standing was starting to be more challenging. Our hope was that on this day, he would have had the strength to stand.

There had been chatter throughout the community about why we chose to get married once he was diagnosed with ALS. Well, to know Alex is to understand that he will address you when need be, properly and respectfully.

After we said our vows, he asked for the microphone and addressed our guests with "Peace and Blessings," a formal greeting he always used. He thanked our guests for being there to witness our union and also challenged them to be true to why they were there. He called out some people in general for being there just to signify and praised those who were there to support us on our journey. When Alex spoke, he didn't have to demand attention from others. People just listened in amazement because of the eloquent manner in which he spoke and because of his vocabulary. Alex also made it a point to acknowledge that when he was diagnosed with ALS, I chose to stick it out with him. He told everyone assembled that he would forever be grateful for being blessed with a queen like me by his side. "She could have easily said no," he said, "but the solid foundation had been laid and our destination had been set."

As I looked around the room, there wasn't a dry eye in sight. Alex openly shared his heart with everyone, and they were receptive to what he said during our wedding ceremony.

As promised, Alex made sure I received the wedding of my dreams. It was most definitely fit for the queen he called me and the queen he treated me like.

From beginning to the end, we were on cloud nine. Our faces had permanent smiles on them, signaling exactly how we were feeling. My Prince Charming made my wildest dreams come true by loving me unconditionally and properly.

4

Hurricane

RESPIRATORY FAILURE

One month and six days after our wedding, around four o'clock in the afternoon, the lives of Alex and Alisha changed forever. I remember Alex saying, "Go, go, go...I can't breathe. Get me to the hospital." I was trying to remain as calm as possible while watching him squirm in the passenger seat.

When we arrived at the hospital, Alex was in distress and struggling to catch his next breath. After getting him settled in the ER, I left the hospital for a few minutes. The Emergency Room doctor called to tell me to get there in the next five minutes because Alex needed to be put on life support due to respiratory failure. *Say what? Come again! What do you mean?* All kinds of questions were swirling through my mind.

Once I was back at the hospital, I turned to his mother and asked her what I should do. Her words to me were, "You are his wife, and I will respect the decision you choose to make." On top of being heavily emotional, I was extremely terrified. From what I had been told, some people never recover from being on life support, so I didn't know what to expect. I wrestled with the what if's, why me and why us. I needed God to explain this one to me.

Agreeing to allow the doctors to put Alex on life support was the most difficult decision I've ever made in my life, but the only one that would save his in that moment. My heart was in my stomach the entire time he was in surgery.

While sitting in the family waiting room, I sent his mother, father, my mother, Nick, Nico and Anthony back to see him first. When I walked in the Critical Care Unit Room 130, my world literally caved in. I saw tubes everywhere. He was hooked up to so many monitors and machines. *Lord, how in the world did we get here* was the only question on my mind.

I cried and cried and cried until I couldn't cry anymore. Alex was heavily sedated and didn't know he was in the world, much less that I was in the room. Even with the greatest support system at my side, I felt helpless. I was angry because we were supposed to still be celebrating our marriage, in the "honeymoon phase." I was confused because I was praying yet God wasn't responding. I needed to talk to Alex. I needed him to tell me what to do and how to handle this situation because at this point, his life was in my hands. I was frustrated, devastated and lost. *What in the world did we do that was so wrong to deserve this?*

The next morning, I pulled my chair up next to his bed, grabbed his hand and cried some more. While praying, the only thing I could utter was Lord please!

I felt a gentle touch on my shoulder from his nurse. She told me she was praying for us and assured me we were going to be ok. With tears in her eyes, she introduced herself to me. Shelly vowed to be there for us, and she kept her promise.

Word spread quickly throughout the unit that we were newlyweds, and every nurse we had showed so much compassion towards us. One even shared her story about losing a loved one to ALS. So, she understood what we were up against, even though our journey was somewhat different.

When he finally came around, Alex looked so frightened and confused. I told him what had taken place. The sad part is he heard me clearly and comprehended what I said but was unable to speak or ask me any questions.

Reading his lips was a major challenge for everyone who entered the room. Alex was a talker and an excellent communicator. He was a wordsmith. He spoke very eloquently with depth and meaning, and every word out of his mouth was carefully chosen for every conversation he had, whether he was speaking to someone young or old. When he spoke, people listened intently to what he had to say. They sought advice from him and valued his opinion.

One of my daily prayers after Alex was diagnosed with ALS was, "Lord, please spare his voice because his voice was such an integral part of who he was." Trust me when I tell you that trying to communicate with him on life support was oh, so difficult.

One evening he was mouthing something to me, and I couldn't understand what he was asking me to do. I struggled to grasp what he was saying and he became upset. Turns out he was asking me to turn off the light. I felt like a complete failure for not being able to figure out something so simple.

Alex was still able to use his hands, so we had to become creative by using a white board with the alphabet on it to communicate. I asked God again, *how did we get here?* Still no answer.

Alex had a tube down his throat that prevented him from being able to communicate, eat or drink. For days I felt guilty for eating even a piece of bread or drinking a glass of water because he was unable to.

After two weeks, Alex got to the point where he was able to breathe on his own. The doctors took him off the vent for minutes at a time, but he still struggled continuously. We were told to consider putting a feeding tube in his stomach so he could get the proper nutrients during this process, as well as a tracheostomy tube in his throat.

I consulted his primary physician and discussed it with our family. Ma Margaret, Nick, Nico and Anthony were very helpful with getting Alex to understand the importance of these artificial forms of life support.

After the procedures were done, Alex asked for a mirror so he could see the hole in his throat. He wasn't as concerned about the feeding tube in his stomach. The look on his face once he saw the hole indicated fear. Yet we both found comfort in knowing there was a possibility of this being a temporary situation. Alex hadn't been able to walk the entire time he was in the Critical Care Unit, or CCU. Physical therapy assisted him with standing, but he was unable to walk due to his being on life support and having a tracheostomy.

Visits from family and friends became a little easier, and Alex was able to talk if his cuff was partially deflated. He wasn't on any dietary restrictions so anything he wanted to eat, he got.

For thirty-one days, I spent the night at the hospital with my husband, sleeping in the most uncomfortable chairs. Our home was literally within walking distance, just five minutes from the hospital, but there was no way I was going to leave him alone. I know some women might have taken a night off here or there just to sleep in their own bed. And I know had I asked his mom or my mom to relieve me for a night or two to provide respite, they would have readily agreed. But there was no way on this earth I was going to leave him. He needed me and God knows I desperately needed him. After sleeping in his hospital room all night, most mornings after leaving the hospital, I could barely make the short drive home and insert the key in our front door before the tears started flowing. While bathing, it was as though the water drops from the shower head and the tears from my eyes were competing to see which could fall more steadily. I cried for many reasons. For one, it really hurt to see Alex lying in a hospital bed, hooked up to any number of machines. Also, it was frustrating to witness Alex, a man known for his eloquent means of expression, unable to speak. But that wasn't it. I was also troubled over knowing my husband was fighting such a formidable foe. Likewise, it truly saddened me to think of the many young children, particularly African American boys, who may never get the chance to learn some life-changing wisdom from him. I cried for Alex's mother, children, siblings, aunts, uncles, cousins and close friends because I knew the void that could possibly be left in their lives ... one day. And it goes without saying that I cried because my heart was absolutely broken. I had finally found the man of my dreams. We had gotten married and vowed to spend the rest of our lives supporting and trusting and respecting and loving each other. Yet who knew the rest of our lives would possibly be shorter than the length of time it takes to graduate from high school...

Of course, my tears didn't flow only in the shower or while I was at home alone. The tissues came out at night as I sat in Alex's hospital room watching over him and praying for him. I'd sit there longing to position myself in the bed with him, just to be even that much closer to him and to hear his heart beating. But of course I couldn't sleep in the bed with him, so the uncomfortable hospital room chair had to suffice. Often as I sat in it, I cried. Sure I'd listen to gospel music, read my Bible, write in my journal and send and receive text messages. I'd even occasionally watch a sitcom, news show or movie on TV. Yet no matter what I was doing, it seemed the tears always forced their way into my routine the way a nosy, annoying coworker puts her two cents into every conversation.

Honestly, I'm convinced I sometimes cried even in my sleep. I know for a fact that I often dreamt of happier times, a world in which there was no ALS, a world in which the only machines my husband had to bother with were our washer and dryer when it was time to do the laundry.

Yet, despite every emotion I was feeling and the fact I was hurting so badly inside as my world crumbled around me, as Alex's wife I still had to appear strong. I had to do it for him. I had to do it for us. And, as crazy as it may sound, I had to do it for me or I just simply wouldn't have been able to function.

I was hurting so bad on the inside. *Lord, why my husband out of all people?* I was still asking questions and receiving no answers.

Our village was amazing and were present daily. Because of them, Alex and I got through that extremely difficult time.

Although Alex was going through a tough time, he still managed to encourage others. He made a post on social media that said, "If I can SMILE with a tube in my throat, I'm sure you can find something to SMILE about and be thankful for. By no means do I want to be here; however, it's part of my journey and I know by SMILING when it seems like I'm at a low point, that may possibly encourage others. So once again, find something in your life to SMILE about and be thankful for. Keep being EXTRAORDINARY."

After spending thirty-one days in CCU, we were advised that the next phase would be rehabilitation. The closest location was about fifty minutes away in Greensboro, N.C., at Moses Cone Hospital. I begged his doctor to allow us to stay a few more days in Salisbury because my birthday was the next day and we wanted to be surrounded by our family. Unfortunately, I had to go home and pack for our next journey.

Angela followed us with flashers on to Greensboro in her car that was packed with our belongings. And understand I mean she rode the ambulance's bumper the entire way. Once we arrived, Suave met us and we were told to stay in the hall until they got Alex situated. When they opened the door, all I saw was a bunch of extra equipment hooked up to him and I lost it. We were never informed about Alex having to start over on the hospital ventilator or about him not being able to eat for another two weeks. We were most definitely going backwards, and someone had some explaining to do. The doctor who decided to take Alex's case was out of town, but we demanded to have some form of communication with him. The hospital was able to schedule a robot call, allowing us to talk via video chat with him. He indicated he'd never had an ALS patient and agreed to taking Alex's case primarily because he'd had the Stem Cell Transplant and believed he could help him get better.

The conversation with the doctor helped to calm Angela's nerves and mine, causing us to feel a tad better about the next thirty days in rehab. Every day I was there by his side, crying more than smiling, stressed out, depressed, hoping and praying that God would turn around our situation. I was praying more and more, with still no response from God. I was hearing from Alex, though. Alex indicated numerous times, "This is part of the process; this is part of the journey." Honestly, I didn't want to hear that. I wanted God to answer me. I wanted God to fix it.

The methods Moses Cone decided to try seemed to be working. Alex was challenged daily. The first day, he was taken off the ventilator for what was supposed to be two hours but stayed off for twice as long. The second day he was taken off the vent for eight hours but stayed off for nine. The third day he was taken off for a scheduled twelve hours but mastered sixteen, the same amount required of him the next day. His doctor looked at Alex with tears in his eyes and called him his "HERO." I called him a fighter, a miracle and an inspiration to many, a man who was making progress daily while keeping a SMILE on his face.

His next challenge was to get up and walk while off the ventilator. His nurses hooked him to the oxygen machine in preparation for what he was set to do. While getting prepped, we went live on Facebook and his message to those watching was, "Peace and Blessings Family. Never give up on yourself regardless of what anyone says. If there is a will, there is a way. You gotta fight sometimes. I will never stop fighting. Life is good. I'm happy to still be alive."

That day Alex walked one hundred feet from his room to the nurses' station and one hundred feet back. The nurses were so proud of the progress he was making and so were we. He was determined. He was tenacious. He was courageous. He was fighting which allowed him the opportunity to return home as expected.

We spent both of our birthdays in the hospital. For mine, Angela and Suave asked Alex for permission to take me out for dinner and tried their best to make it one of my best birthdays ever. For Alex's birthday, family and friends came and we had decorations everywhere. Even the nurses joined in and celebrated with us.

Not long after, we retuned home to a house filled with love from family and friends who were very excited to see us but also the progress that Alex had made. We also returned to a home filled with a hospital bed, oxygen concentrator, ventilator and trache supplies. Everyday we received an overflow of medical supplies that we never knew existed. On top of that therapist and nurses who were complete strangers providing twenty-four-hour care for Alex.

We were still in our honeymoon phase with limited privacy in our own home but made the best tasting lemonade with the lemons we were given.

APOLOGIES

Despite everything Alex and I went through, what hurt me more than anything was hearing him apologize because he thought he was a burden to me. There were times when my physical strength far exceeded what my mind thought I was capable of doing. For example, one time Alex and I were preparing for an early Baptist Hospital appointment at the ALS Clinic.

We got up extra early. I fed and dressed Alex. His bags were packed, and our newly purchased SUV was loaded. As we began the transition from his wheelchair to our vehicle, I realized that getting Alex into the SUV was going to be much harder than I imagined. The more I tried to lift him, the heavier he felt, which caused my legs to weaken. Mind you, Alex was on a ventilator and hooked up to oxygen, so his mobility was very limited, meaning he couldn't help me get him into the SUV.

As I placed him on the side of the door, I cried and apologized because I felt like an absolute failure for not being able to complete the simple task of getting him into the car. The more I prayed and asked God for strength, the more I cried. Eventually, God blessed me with the right amount of strength to lift all one hundred forty-five pounds of Alex into the car.

Once we were both buckled in and I pulled off, Alex reached for my hand and apologized for taking me through what he considered to be too much. I am strongest when he smiles at me, but I am weakest when he apologizes to me. Hearing him say "I'm Sorry" hurts me more than anything.

With tears in both of our eyes, we reminded each other that this episode was part of the process and part of our journey. Our ride to Winston Salem was unusually quiet because each of us was feeling as though we'd failed each other in some way. As we were driving it began raining, and we began smiling because it was another indication of the beautiful storm our marriage was surviving.

5

Tides & Waves

CHATTER

"Believe it or not, some people had the audacity to ask mutual friends of ours—and some family members—why Alex waited until he got sick to propose to me." Others openly questioned why I married Alex knowing he had a terminal illness. People asked these questions and said hurtful things without even understanding the foundation that had been formed between Alex and me.

Some of these people were our so-called friends. They smiled in our faces and, when they saw me without Alex, asked how he was doing. Yet and still they were having sidebar conversations with others who came back and told us.

When it came to our feelings, Alex and I were on two separate pages. I would wear my hurt and pain on my sleeve, while he would let words and actions roll off his back. Instead of confronting most of the people I felt were verbally attacking us and not being true friends, I just cut them off and never looked back.

I did learn one thing: The same way favor isn't fair; neither was being the chosen one. First I was chosen by God for Alex. Then, after a series of questions and conversations with God to confirm I was the one for him, Alex chose me. I remember once, Alex's mom told me that all kinds of women were contacting her on Facebook Messenger to ask whether Alex was serious about me and if we were a couple.

Many of those women were simply looking to get married, to say they had a "husband." As I think about it now, most of those same women likely would have left Alex once he could no longer walk, after he could no longer take them out for a night on the town.

And, if they didn't leave then, most of them certainly would have bolted out the door once he could no longer dress himself. And we won't even talk about them breaking Olympic records sprinting for the nearest exit once Alex could no longer bathe or even wipe himself. Yet I did it all with a smile on my face because he was my husband, the one God created just for me. He was the one who changed my life and mended my broken heart from loves gone bad in a mere twenty-one days.

OUR VILLAGE

There's an African proverb that states, "It takes a village to raise a child." Thankfully, we experienced the true meaning of this proverb as adults after Alex was diagnosed with ALS. When Alex received the devastating diagnosis, we were blessed with the most amazing village. Our family and friends stepped up to the plate, putting aside much of their personal agendas and lives to ensure we were taken care of. Our "Village" was composed of phenomenal and extraordinary people—the kind you would most definitely want on your team and in your life if you were going through.

THROUGH IT ALL

Pastor Timothy Bates

I can't fully explain the inspiration, strength and love I personally witnessed as Alex and Alisha traveled along their journey.

You two never ceased to amaze me and definitely made the storm Beautiful. Wow!

I remember at Essie Mae Foxx's funeral when I noticed Alex having difficulty coming off the stage. He said, "brother, just hold my hand."

I also remember the day Alex told me at the car wash, "Bruh, I have ALS but it doesn't have me." It was as though he was questioning whether I was ready to fight with him.

Through it all, you two partied your way through—even with a great surprise party celebrating the life of Alex Clark.

Despite your trials, you continued blessing youth with scholarships and life-changing advice while sacrificing your time and more. Thanks for the gift you even gave to my wife and me.

Together you laughed and cried your way through. Alisha, I remember the day you said quite seriously to me, "Take him with you," because he'd been getting on your nerves.

At times you sang your way through. "Keep Risin' To The Top". You even danced your way through. What a Beautiful Storm.

Most of all, you prayed your way through. The day that brother prayed for me, I witnessed the power of a believing wife, and that's all I'm going to say about that.

The wedding topped it off when I saw Grandma Minnie walk you, Alisha, down the aisle and witnessed as you two said "I Do" before you made a profound commitment by telling Alex, "I loved you before you had ALS, so I will love you with ALS." Beautiful!!!

You two are a beautiful example of I DO and unconditional love. Because of you, I am a better person. I'm inspired, encouraged and motivated to be all I can *while I can*. I love the Clarks and the Beautiful Storm.

ETERNALLY GRATEFUL

Pastor Rick Galloway

One thing I love about God is how He connects our lives with people to whom we least expect. I am eternally grateful for the connection He made with me and Alex Clark. God allowed our paths to cross and form a genuine bond between men.

My connection with Alex connected me to others I would have never met, as he brought people together from all walks of life.

Men, especially African American men or brothers as we're often called, can be skeptical of each other when they first meet. Such was the case for Alex and me. We were cordial to each other, but we had to feel each other out. Over time, we both recognized we were real, strong black men who cared about people, especially our people. In my estimation, Alex was gifted and brilliant.

He had a unique ability to connect men and galvanize them around a common goal. He pulled things out of you that you didn't know existed. He believed in challenging people to help them grow. He would not let people settle for mediocrity but instead pushed them to do their best.

Alex was like E.F. Hutton: When he spoke, *everybody* listened. He was a man of wisdom. I never met a man like Alex with an uncanny ability to have you hanging onto every word he spoke. I will never forget the time Alisha was celebrating Alex's life. He spoke at the end of the celebration for one whole hour and nobody moved. We sat like children, absorbing every word. It was simply an amazing moment in time.

Alex told me that we must deal with the enemy within that keeps us from reaching our God-given destiny. We must face the enemy and overcome the enemy by pushing through the obstacles and challenges we face. We must fight.

It was late last year when I was going through a tough season in my ministry and I was summoned by Alex to come see him. He told Alisha he needed to see me that day; however, in classic Alex fashion, he poured into me exactly *what I needed* that day. I arrived empty yet left with a full cup, energized and ready to move mountains.

Alex was a pusher and wouldn't let you give up. He was a trailblazer who didn't mind ruffling feathers to achieve a goal. Alex was about living life without regrets. Living a life of purpose.

When I think of A.L.E.X, these words immediately come to mind:

*A-Available. L-Lover. E-Encourager. X-X-rayer.
C-Courageous. L-Lion. A-Assigned. R-Raw. K-King.*

Alex, thank you for having a profound impact on my life in just a short time. God always gives us what we need when we need it. The dream still lives. We must carry the legacy. I will do my part.

DIVINE CONNECTION

Angela Alford

As I reflect on my journey with the Clarks, I have to say our initial connection was very unique. People may question the connection and not understand it, but that's the beautiful thing about divine connections. Most of the time we don't understand how or why divine connections happen. It's not important to focus on trying to "figure it out." Instead, you should just roll with it.

We never know why we are placed in the lives of others, and vice versa. I never thought I would meet a new brother and sister this late in life. You see, growing up I always heard that you meet your lifelong friends in college. Although that is also true, I have to say my relationship with Alex and Alisha is nothing short of a miracle. Through the connection, I have had the opportunity to bond with other amazing people who are now family. The truth is, we have to understand that our life is not our own and that we were born to serve God and others.

This connection all started from a nice gesture, which comes naturally to me. That nice gesture turned into a lifelong bond, one I now lovingly and proudly call family.

From the calls and text messages any time day or night, sometimes not knowing or understanding what was taking place or what the outcome would be, this journey and process has helped to strengthen my faith in unimaginable ways.

We watched God show up and completely turn situations around, sometimes quickly and other times not as fast as we desired. No matter how long it took, we always knew who was in control. God always knew where Alex and Alisha stood as a couple and where we stood as a support system.

It's important to have people around you that can go to God and touch heaven on your behalf. Alex and Alisha will never know the amount of silent prayers I sent up while in their presence, how many hours I fasted for a miracle or how many times, while feeding or suctioning Alex or handling whatever was needed, I whispered prayers during the process and how many times I watched God move and change the whole scenario just like that. Yes, I know others have always prayed as well, but I think I'm God's favorite.

I remember one night I was so worn in my spirit because it seemed nothing we did worked or made the situation any better for Alex. He was frustrated. Alisha was frustrated. I knew he was tired, and I wanted to fix it but couldn't. I remember going home and calling my brother Nick and saying, "I don't know what to do. I'm supposed to be strong. I'm supposed to be the backbone, and I'm lost." As tears rolled down my face, I continued, "I don't have the right words to say, and I don't know what to do."

The conversation with Nick that night changed my perception of everything. I gained the courage and strength to continue on the journey, being the backbone for my sister while remembering my truth and purpose.

Okay. Enough of the spiritual part. Let's get to the other part of how we earned the name "Clatchet" from the "Melanated Genius" himself. So, with love comes protection. Ain't no protection like that of Angela R. Alford, when it comes to her favorite people—no matter who you are. Alex had to be moved to Moses Cone Hospital in Greensboro, N.C. We asked all of the clarifying questions about travel and purpose before we left Novant Hospital in Salisbury, N.C. We were told all of these wonderful things were going to happen once we got to Moses Cone.

Now you know people always sell you the outcome, but not the process. Welp, they found out quickly that Alisha and I were not the ones for this nonsense. I was following behind the ambulance with my flashers on, and the paramedic had the nerve to tell Alisha to call me to say I needed to slow down because I could still get a ticket even though I was following behind the ambulance. I told Alisha ok and guess what? I kept right on driving fast.

When we arrived at the hospital, of course I had to park in a different lot and couldn't follow the ambulance to its destination. They tried to tell me I had to wait in the lobby and that I couldn't go back with Alex and Alisha. You already know that went over like a lead balloon. I said, simply, "I'm going with her." When we got to the room, we were told we needed to wait outside. They had Alex in the room talking to him with the door shut, not telling us anything. Umm. Hello. We have questions, people.

By this time, we were angry. We felt responsible and didn't know what these people were doing to Alex. We wanted to get in that room right then. We needed to see what was happening.

When we finally got in, we noticed they had taken him off his personal machine and put him on the hospital ventilator and other equipment, talking about the process. We were upset because we had not heard of this beforehand. I remember thinking and feeling like they were taking him backwards and that was not ok.

We were fired up, and everyone knew it. The staff tried, but no one could give us the answers we desired. As you know, this was not ok. The staff members were saying things like, "The doctor is not here and won't be back until tomorrow." Negative. Long story short, the coolest thing happened. Dr. Robot came in. It's amazing where technology has taken us. Yes, the doctor was an actual robot. Upright, he stood about four feet, and he moved easily around the hospital. The interaction with the robotic doctor helped calm our nerves. Better yet, our fears. The truth is we were afraid.

Alex stayed at Moses Cone for thirty days, and I was there almost every day. We had so much fun during this time. We would all gather, Nick, Alisha, Suave and me, at the room for "round bed" deep discussions. We celebrated both Alex's and Alisha's birthdays during his stay, and we also had moments of prayer. Man, we can take any space and turn it into an atmosphere of celebration and excitement! I'm talking about decorations, food, music *and* guests.

During the discussions, businesses were born, motivation was sent forth and inspiration, love and accountability were always the cornerstone. While at Moses Cone, it blessed me even more to see men!

Not just any men, but men who were unafraid and unashamed to be vulnerable. They will never know how that impacted my life. This not only happened at Moses Cone, but throughout the process.

During Alex's thirty days at Moses Cone, he made so much progress and things were moving in a positive direction. Each day it was so exciting to hear and see the new things he was doing. Breathing longer on his own. Walking further distances. It was usually the highlight of my day to receive an update from Alisha. Everything at Moses Cone was good.

The time came when the conversation turned to Alex going home. The nurse said for that to happen, anyone helping to provide care would have to be trained. Well that meant Nick, Suave and I had to learn how to suction along with other responsibilities. As afraid as I was to try, I did. Let's just say I earned my nursing license from Alex Clark. Let's also say Suave got on my nerves because he "thought" he was already a nurse *and* a doctor. It seemed no matter which hospital Alex was sent to, Moses Cone or Novant, Alisha and I always managed to meet new friends. At Moses Cone, the cafeteria manager became our aunt, and it was a joy to walk downstairs to see her and be touched by her positive energy. She was such a blessing and took great care of us.

I would be remiss if I didn't talk about how amazing Nick and Suave are as men, exemplifying what it means to have your brother's back. Don't mistake what I'm saying. Others were there for Alex too, but I had the opportunity to watch and experience Nick and Suave on an almost daily basis. It's funny, because both of them act cool and collected, but when it came to Alex, they turned into different people. Overprotective is an understatement.

One night, Alisha and I got in trouble with Nick because we were not moving fast enough to get the door opened for Alex's arrival. The funniest part about it was we were really nervous. Ok, for full disclosure when we left the hospital, Nick and Alex were in Nick's car and Alisha and I were together. Alisha and I left first to get to the house before them. You know us. We started talking and thanking God for allowing Alex to get well enough to be released and time just passed. When we got to the porch, we couldn't find the correct key. The next thing we knew, we saw the headlights coming down the street and I started laughing. Alisha said, "You better stop laughing. Here they come." We were nervous, grew quiet and made our way into the house. As soon as Nick got out he said, "Ya'll don't have that door opened yet?" We didn't say a word. We just went in the house and started scrambling around in silence.

I forgot to mention helping to prepare Alex for Mr. Byrd's funeral which was Alisha's grandfather. Everything was going well until Suave and I put Alex in the car. He was sharp as a tack. I closed his door and was getting ready to make my way across the street to my car when everything took a wrong turn. I don't know what happened, but I ended up on the asphalt in the middle of the street. Alex was so concerned, and according to Suave he looked like he was going to jump out of the car to save me. Suave asked Alex, "Where are you going?" Alex responded by laughing and saying, "I don't know."

There were times when Alex would do so well with eating and talking. Because he was eating so well, of course he gained weight. The increased weight changed the game for us to the point where we found ourselves in situations when we almost dropped Alex's heavy behind. We would communicate the struggle to Alex and he would give us a look that made me laugh, which made me lose more strength, making matters even worse. He asked one time, "What, y'all just gonna drop me?" But The Lord covered us, provided strength and we never dropped him.

There is so much more I could share about this journey. What I will say is my life will never be the same and the growth that occurred in me will never be wasted. I learned so much about relationships in different capacities, but the greatest capacity was how a woman is supposed to love and serve her husband. Alisha is the epitome of a virtuous woman. Every day was not easy. At times I sat and watched in amazement the strength and courage Alisha possessed. Alisha is nothing short of amazing. Like a lot of women would have, she could have decided not to stand by Alex. But God. Her latter will be so much greater, and I am blessed to be close enough to witness it manifest.

THE FOUR QUEENS

Veleria Levy

I've struggled with this because not only was Alex Clark my friend and my self-proclaimed brother-in-law; he was a mentor to my son. Being a single mom is a struggle. But no matter what you project on the outside, Alex always had a way of knowing. Before I even said anything; he knew. That is kind of how our relationship went. He always was the one that used his "third eye" and asked you to think beyond what you could even imagine for yourself. That is the reason why he made such a good mentor and friend.

Our relationship started when he married my sister in spirit, Alisha. She and I had known each other only a short time but found ourselves becoming fast friends. When she spoke of Alex, her whole spirit changed. You not only could sense it. You could feel it. You just knew. When we met, I was ready to give him the riot act as sisters do, but you could just see and feel the ties were strong between them. They had a true connection. Then the magic began to happen! They started making their mark on the world and you couldn't help but get on board. Alex would say, "If you don't have to be with me just get out of the way," or something like that LOL. I always knew he was telling me to get on board. See, you could always tell it was a master plan that he was walking, and everything had a place in the plan.

In 2016 when I decided to run for elected office, I went over to talk with Alex and Alisha. See, I've been told I'm not Black enough, I'm a pawn for the man, I'm the token African American, etc. It has always bothered me, and I've always tried to fit into those two worlds, not quite sure about either of them. But when I decided to step up and run for office, I needed to answer those questions: Who Am I and why am I running for elected office? Well, I had the "Why am I running" part down cold! I knew exactly why, all of the numbers, the issues, etc. Well, I thought I did... (This is where people who know Alex will start to laugh, LOL.) So like I said, I arranged to speak with them about my campaign, since both of them grew up in Rowan County and I was from Virginia. "Sit down, Queen," Alex said after I entered their home. Anyone else would have known how to handle that, but I laughed because I didn't know I was a Queen. Hell, no one had ever called me that and meant it from a place of genuine respect.

At one point in my life, I was a queen—pageant queen that is. I've held several titles over my life and enjoyed modeling and acting. My life has always been about appearances and doing what people expected me to do, while never quite understanding what I was doing and what I really wanted to do. How do you answer a question about who you are when you don't even know yourself?

Not until Alex continued addressing me as Queen did I start to really seriously ask myself "Who am I beyond what's on paper? Who am I beyond the makeup, clothes, shoes, bags and the career? Just who am I? At first when we were talking about my campaign, I still was "plastic." I knew what to say, what to do and how to say it. But Alex wasn't buying it. Not at all. "Queen," he said, "who are you?" I'm telling you. I had my ready-made, set answers and he was having none of it.

Having lived the life of a pageant queen, model and actress, you just can't beat me with the right answer. I keep them on me at all times. But he wasn't looking for the "right answer." He was looking for me. Hell, who knew I didn't even know me? My voice cracked and a tear fell down my face. I didn't want to be real. I didn't want to be upfront. I mean, who wants to do that? Who wants to be exposed? Alex said," You have to peel off the layers, sis, because real people will know you're not being real. You deserve to be you, and the community deserves to know who they're really backing." Over the next few months I did a deep dive into me, trying to decide just how many layers I wanted to peel back. I wondered whether I could just give the world two or three layers and keep the rest, LOL. Nope! Again, Alex was having none of it.

After reading the "Four Queens" written by Alex Clark again, it was then when I realized I am the Queen of Hearts, Queen on Diamonds,

Queen of Spades, Queen of Clubs; Hell, I am the Complete Queen and I understand the powers of my crown and how to use each and apply each one in my life.

Our conversations grew, and so did my faith in the journey. Yes, I was running for office. But I was also running to find myself. Allowing yourself to be vulnerable is hard and can be a bitter pill to swallow—especially when your life has been based on appearances.

Alex pulled no punches and told me I had to get in front of some of the things I thought made me flawed. Those were things that made me who I am, he said, and I needed to embrace the scars instead of covering them from the world with makeup. So I started peeling back the layers and letting people see the real me—the real Veleria Levy. I talked about being a single mom with some challenges and making some bad decisions, in part because I was blinded by what I thought was love. I talked about being sexually abused as a child and raped in college. I talked about being caught between two worlds: being black, but not black enough for some and too black for others. I cried. I laughed. I emotionally ate. I cried and laughed some more. NEVER at any time did Alex look at me with a judgmental face. He continued calling me Queen and told me to keep going. He was right. It was hard, but it was so worth it.

In 2016 as a candidate I stood up. I spoke out. I met with people, talked about the issues, talked about my why and shared my personal story. Yes, some people judged me, but more people embraced me. Me??!! Vulnerable. Flawed. Scared but Strong! Strong because I was learning to stand in my truth! Alex shared his story and made no excuses. That is what made him Alex, and that is why people respect him and all of his journey.

I listened intently to him, to his advice. I knew the numbers were not in my favor, but I ran and ran hard. I spoke out, sometimes being called the Angry Black Woman. But it was ok because I was standing in my truth. Although I lost the election, I found myself. I found my fight and found the Queen inside and there was no turning back after that! I was officially an activist, and not just "playing one on TV" LOL Through all of this, I became a part of "The Family," an inner circle of sorts. As part of the family, the real journey started as I continued to discover the layers I'd been covering and masking. It was and still is a constant battle between who I think I am and who I really am. It was and still is a perpetual struggle to raise a young black man in this crazy world, teaching him how to embrace his truth in a world that strives to constantly keep him down and in "his place."

Alex and Alisha started Gemstones & COMPASS, mentoring organizations for young black boys and girls. I started out on the Board of Directors and immediately knew their mentorship program was the perfect place for my son. We jumped in and never turned back! Joseph Earl looked forward to going and so did my dad. COMPASS was for men and boys only and gave my dad an avenue to discuss some of his childhood and the civil rights movement with not only Joseph Earl but with other kids as well. They both loved it! COMPASS gave my son the backbone he needed to feel comfortable with his blackness in a world that wants him to be invisible.

Over the years, the slogan Black Lives Matter became real to my son. He was becoming a teenager as many of us simultaneously celebrated President Barack Obama as the country's first black President while being confronted with the ugly truths of police brutality and white supremacy. It was a perfect time for COMPASS to help him sort through it all. I am his mother and I love him, but he needed other black Men to help him with the feelings he was experiencing as a teenager—specifically as a black teenager.

The stories he tells about the "COMPASS Village" are priceless. They deal with all the aspects of COMPASS: Confident, Optimistic, Motivated, Persistent, Assertive, Studious and Successful. They prepare our youth for the future—the good and the bad, wins and losses and acceptances and challenges. Alex's relationship with the COMPASS kids was one of mutual respect and admiration. I have so many stories to share, but the one that left the greatest impact on me was the time during a disagreement with my son when he caught my hand as I raised it to spank him. I called Alisha and told her and she told Alex. Alex told me to drop Joseph Earl off the next day to hang out with him. I did, and they had a day of "growth and understanding" LOL. Alex asked a few of his friends from prison to come by, and they had a long, hard talk with my son about grabbing my hand and disrespecting women. (I guess you could call it a subtle version of "Beyond Scared Straight.") Although Joseph Earl and I can laugh about it now, it was really a pivotal time in his life, one that he'll never forget.

Learning to be a stronger advocate for myself allowed me to be a better advocate for others. Growing up with strong black mentors will allow Joseph Earl to be a better man and mentor to others. "Iron Sharpens Iron". We are both stronger, wiser and ultimately better because we allowed ourselves to be vulnerable and to step out of our comfort zone thanks to Alex Clark

THE HERO I KNOW

Joseph Earl Levy, III
COMPASS Man of the Year

I don't know where I would be without Mr. Alex. I was hanging with the wrong people and heading down the wrong path when I met him, and he taught me how to be a king and direct my own path.

Mr. Alex didn't help only me. He helped many people in my community, becoming a real-life hero to everybody he met whether he knew them or not. He never worried about himself. Instead, he always took care of others. He was strict because he wanted the best for everyone he met.

I am a Compass man, which means I need to be a leader who strives to realize his full potential and never gives up. That is what he is doing right now not giving up because he had a Compass Mindset, meaning he was CONFIDENT, OPTIMISTIC, MOTIVATED PERSISTENT, ASSERTIVE, STUDIOUS and SUCCESSFUL. Those seven words epitomize what it means to be a Compass Man. That is the path Mr. Alex laid for people, the path he created for me.

Thank you, Mr. Alex, for everything you did for me.

KING ALEX: OUR HEALER

Pastor Anthony Smith

If Alex Clark were born a thousand years ago, he would have been a king with his own kingdom, a queen, a standing army, a royal court, a school of philosophers and scientists and a battalion of artists and musicians. He would have ruled justly with mercy and knowledge. He would have reminded people of their excellence while sitting under the "Elder Tree" to share life-giving wisdom with the village's youth. The kind of wisdom that makes one more knowledgeable than one could ever conceive. If you use only a tiny fraction of your imagination, you can easily see that Alex would have been a dope king.

However, we are in the early part of the 21st Century, a time when many don't remember their excellence or their greatness. It is in this time, not a thousand years ago, that Alex, the would-be king, flowered and shined. In these times and in this place, we don't have kings ruling the land or our political systems. Nonetheless, Alex was still a king., While it's true he didn't rule over people, it's also true that he had a queen. Her name is Alisha Byrd-Clark, and trust me when I say she's powerful in her own way. Alex helped mobilize us like an army, a Circle of Kings. He convened a battalion of artists and musicians—Firewater, et al—and he reminded us of our excellence and greatness via COMPASS. Make no mistake about it: Alex was a king.

He was also a community healer. His words and presence could heal the broken places of our collective psyche, damaged by centuries of white supremacy that tried to teach black people that they are inferior. Alex helped us remember that we are _not_ inferior, which is very healing and powerful. He was adept at fetching, or Sankofa, and taught us how to reach back to fetch the wisdom, principles and knowledge of our ancestors and bring that to the present in hopes of creating a better future.

Alex was a Melanated Genius who loved his people. Black people. He saw our greatness when many of us could not. He reminded us that we all had black genius in us. Or as Alex would coin the phrase: melanated genius. For him to simply add the word 'melanated' to the word genius was to set ablaze a spiritual and cultural revolt against the status quo. It was a revolt because too many of us can conceive of genius in only non-melanated bodies. Alex was like, "Nah, bruh. We have genius in us, too." Great genius. All we had to do, Alex taught us, is look within ourselves and back to the history of our ancestors. We all possess genius and the ability to be creative, innovative, artistic, entrepreneurs and cultural revolutionaries.

Alex's legacy is of a king and a healer. The most potent work he did was remind us that, like our ancestors, we are all royalty. Not just him. All of our brothers are kings. All of our sisters are queens. He taught and showed us that we all can rule with our own unique melanated genius in this place and in this time. Thank you, King Alex.

FAMILY

Dr. Nicole Sherrill-Jamison

Family is not always biological. After hearing this, I began to question everything I'd learned as a child—all the way into adulthood. Alex Clark embraced everyone in which he came into contact. His words pierced your soul, making you want to learn more to expand your knowledge. My knowledge expanded drastically as a result of interacting with Alex Clark.

The wedding of Alex and Alisha brought together people who knew little about each other. It was a great challenge for me because of my uneasiness with trusting unfamiliar people. The real challenge came when it was time to prepare for the wedding. Even the wedding itself was challenging. However, my love for Alex and Alisha helped me understand the importance of being open and embracing new ideas, new things, etc.

Even so, this was new for me. Throughout the wedding and beyond, this group of individuals that I met as a result of their union became a Village, a Family. Again, this was strange to me because my perception of family centers biological connections. That's neither here nor there now, because thanks to Alex, I welcomed the newness of who I was about to become—especially within the construct of "family."

You see, Alex's battle with ALS affected many people in different ways. He was a book of knowledge, a virtual "walking encyclopedia," that sparked life in so many. As I learned more and more about the illness and Alex, I wanted to know more. Alex had a way with words. He could take the simplest word and use it in a context that you never knew, sending you flying to dictionary.com on your cell phone so you could understand it enough to confidently add it to *your* vocabulary. So, when the word family came up, I was challenged and I accepted it.

Witnessing his life change as a result of ALS helped me understand more about the importance of connection. Connection not so much as interaction, but as a bond. Each day was a challenge for Alex, requiring the Village to assist where and when needed. Accessibility is a word that is connected to Family. Families have to be accessible when needed. Experiencing this family village truly impacted my life. Our village had to be ready, willing and able to meet challenges whenever they presented themselves. Alex would often say, "family does what has to be done when the time comes." Well, the time came many times, and our bond grew stronger and stronger.

Of course, we all have our own personality, and at times the village of personalities didn't quite mesh. Nonetheless, as a family we knew what was expected and needed, and we got the job done. As time continued, we stuck like glue. We loved on each other and were present for each other—all of which occurred because of one strong person—Alex. Getting to know Alex taught me the importance of family. Listening to his words of encouragement and watching his interactions with Alisha and other people was inspiring. I found family, unconditional and true.

The bond we developed through assisting Alex is out of this world. There wasn't a moment that Alisha called or Alex summoned and no one came. We developed a kinship like no other. There were times when I'd visit just to support Alex and Alisha. Every time I stopped by, I left with an even better understanding of the role a family plays.

The life lessons instilled in me will persist even though Alex has transitioned. Listening to him speak was like listening to an elder provide direction on what to do after his or her passing to ensure the family stayed together. The gatherings we had taught us the importance of connecting by sharing. We'd meet, eat, talk, laugh and cry. There were days we'd sit and pray. WOW!!! Our sense of family was very strong.

I remember when Alex first became ill. There was nothing we wouldn't do for him. Every time he was hospitalized, we were all there willing to do our part to make life better for Alex and Alisha. If there was something—anything—I could do, I wanted to be available for my family. Remember, my idea of family was people to whom you are related by blood, a notion that was challenged as I grew to know and love Alex and Alisha. I now know that we were brought together to demonstrate the meaning of family in our community. I will be thankful, always, for our unbreakable bond.

We are Family/Village

MY BROTHER'S KEEPER

Nick Means

I had the pleasure of meeting Alex shortly after he came home from his journey, and we instantly connected. His story reminded me of the guys I ran with and looked up to when I was growing up, but there was something different about him. He seemed to have figured it out. Life, that is. While everyone else seemed to be doing things for show, to be heard and seen, it appeared he wanted simply for his presence to be felt. His sole purpose was to educate, empower and inspire everyone to do better.

Our relationship began as two men, among many, working in our community to make it better, yet morphed into something that I'll cherish for the rest of my life. We would see each other at local schools while volunteering with Man Up and at our Think Tank events put on by Tsunami, a local group of community advocates of which I was a part. It eventually blossomed into a relationship by which we checked on each other to see how the other was doing. The ironic part is he unwittingly ALWAYS reached out to me when I needed him most. I'd be feeling low or going through something and out of the blue he'd send me a text saying, "Peace, lil bro. It's big bro. Keep being EXTRAORDINARY."

I was literally flying by the seat of my pants and didn't have any sense of purpose, direction or motivation when GOD brought Alex into my life.

I was dealing with some relationships that had taken a turn for the worse, and I didn't have much structure and purpose. Alex and Alisha provided the family, structure and love that I needed. Alex and Alisha were my reintroduction to love. They showed me what unconditional love looks like and what it means to be true to ourselves.

One night I got a call from Alisha saying Alex was rushed to the hospital and wasn't doing well. I got to the hospital and found Alisha sitting outside the emergency room alone and terrified. Alex had gone into respiratory failure and was on a ventilator. That was the turning point in our relationship and in a journey that would last until my brother took his last breath.

That night, Anthony Smith and I stood over Alex in his hospital room and prayed and told him we needed him to fight so he could continue doing his work and fulfilling his mission, as we couldn't do it without him.

The next few days/weeks were a struggle. After Alex regained consciousness, it was virtually impossible to read his lips with the ventilator in his mouth. Nico and I talked to Alex about having a tracheostomy, as we felt it would make communication easier and prolong his life.

Alex decided to do it but was unable to talk for some time after the surgery so reading lips became a skill we all mastered. Alex's hospital stint was sixty-one days if I remember correctly, and there weren't many days, if any, that I didn't see him. We were family now, and we were all willing to do what it took to make this transition and new life as comfortable for him as we could.

Over the years, Alex and I would sit in the room and have our music battles, similar to the Instagram battles artists are having today due to COVID-19. However, we weren't playing our original songs, lol. I'm chuckling as I write this because sometimes one of us would play a song and the other would say, "Get out of my head. I was going to play that one next."

We were connected on so many levels that most would have thought we'd known each other our entire lives. Hospital personnel actually thought I was his brother because they saw me so much. It felt like we were brothers, and we loved each other as though we truly were. I'll never forget him telling me, "you can't choose who you're related to, but you can choose your family." I'm grateful that he, Alisha, Momma Margaret, Pops, Shawn, Hen and the kids all chose me because my life is better because of them.

When I think of our time together, I can't help but smile and be grateful. There are so many gems (quotes) he dropped on me that I've saved in my phone as notes, and I actually have some recordings of him speaking on a few occasions that I'll never forget. Reading his words, seeing his face and hearing his voice give me a sense of peace when I need it most.

Alex showed me what sacrifice, determination and loyalty looked like up close and in person. He sacrificed the time he had left on earth, committed to leaving our community better than he found it. His determination to be an inspiration for all of the Melanated Geniuses and Melanted Beauties, despite his condition, showed his loyalty to the cause.

As he always said, "I stand on TRUTH, so I'm not worried about anything else because TRUTH doesn't need anything else because it stands on its own."

That's what my brother did. HE STOOD ON HIS OWN

SECOND OPINION

Andre & Bose Clodfelter

July 4, 2017, was an interesting day, the one when I met Alisha, who I now affectionately call my sister/cousin. I was introduced to Alisha by Alex at the annual family reunion cookout which also happened to be her birthday.

I would never have thought that day would be the start of Andre and I being a part of a Beautiful Storm. Alex, Alisha and I talked for a while and agreed to have dinner the next day. We met at the restaurant, and we started ordering our food.

I remember Alisha telling Alex she'd give up eating certain foods if he'd incorporate some chicken into his diet. Alex discussed his ALS diagnosis with Andre and me, and I suggested he travel to Chicago for a second opinion. I told him I'd research the best doctor in the area and would book his flight. He seemed so hopeful over the prospect of talking to another doctor and receiving a better prognosis, and we were as well. I went back to our hotel and started researching immediately, as it was etched in our minds that we needed to find someone who could effectively treat ALS.

A few days later we returned to Illinois but the research continued. I just had to locate a specialist. I finally found a renowned doctor at the University of Chicago Hospital who specializes in ALS treatment. I called Alex to get his information and make an appointment. Then I scheduled flights for Alex and Alisha and they prepared to come to Chicago.

Andre was so excited to meet them at the airport so we could get some answers about what was going on with his body. The first night we wanted to make sure they had some good Chicago food, because all Chicagoans feel our food is the best in the country.

The next day Alex was scheduled for an early-morning appointment. I was nervous because of the traffic and thought we'd d be late, but we managed to make it right on time. We met with the doctor and I took the lead as his big little sister.

I told the doctor that I was his sister, which enabled me to remain in the room as the doctor examined him. We were praying and hopeful that perhaps this was a misdiagnosis. Maybe this was MS instead of ALS.

The doctor confirmed that Alex did, in fact, have ALS and offered alternative options such as stem cell treatment. I looked at him, he gave me a look and I said "we are fighting this." We left the hospital with a new sense of hope. Stem cell treatment would be the next step in our fight against ALS. We talked about nutrition, and I started giving him SSS Tonic. He didn't like it, but he took it and joked about it being punishment

The research began again, but we had to add some fun. I thought it would be a good idea to go to downtown Chicago and stay along Magnificent Mile for a couple of days so they could enjoy the city while we put together our plan to get Alex stem cell treatment.

Before going downtown, we got couples' massages and boy was that a funny, painful experience. We all left the massage hurting, and Alex said we'd been assaulted. We laughed and laughed about the painful couples' massage.

We headed downtown and began to show them Chicago's famous sites. We took a boat ride on Lake Michigan and walked on the pier. We had some great conversations full of knowledge and love. After spending a couple of days in downtown Chicago, we returned home and started calling places that specialized in stem cell treatments and reading personal testimonies about their success with ALS patients.

We were hopeful and inspired to take on this ugly disease, ALS. We began planning based on the location, price and how we could finance it—even if that meant raising the money. We all recognized that day we had to launch an all-out war against ALS, and we were up for the challenge.

CELLI

Neil (Suave) Blair

In the beginning, me and my bro "King" didn't like each other. We never said it then, but fast forward to 2018 and that's probably what makes our story, our bond, a true love story. And YEA, I LOVE MY BROTHER, ALEX "KING" CLARK.

I went to federal prison in 2001 and was assigned to a unit where I first met INFINITE (Alex.). Some hometown friends I grew up with were already there. One of them was cool with Ron G and INFINITE (Alex), so that's how I met Alex. Our introduction was brief, but we would get to know each and grow our relationship over the next five years.

In the federal prison system, in every prison all over the United States, there's a four o'clock stand up count, preceded by mail call. I had started accepting mail for some of the guys I was cool with who were at work, in their rooms or maybe watching TV at the time. Attendance at mail call wasn't mandatory, so on this day I decided I would call INFINITE (Alex) by his government name, Alex Clark, which is what the commanding officer (CO) called us while distributing mail. So, I just repeated what the CO called him, Alex Clark.

I honestly didn't know this was going to be a big deal, but at the time I didn't care. So, I fueled it by continuing to call him Alex Clark. He was pissed, so pissed that we literally almost got into a fight—all because I refused to respect what INFINITE was asking of me, which was not to call him by his government name. For one, I didn't know him well enough to call him by any other name but the name he told me. Secondly, it was about RESPECT.

Later that day he came up to me and said, "PEACE GOD, let me holla at you," and our brother-ship started from there. He basically let me know in true Alex Clark fashion that I was wrong. He pointed out that everyone calls me Suave, which is what I want to be called. Then he asked me how I would feel if he called me Neil and I asked him not to call me that but he continued doing so. How would I feel about him? Respect begets respect. I told him I get it and he was right. I apologized and from that day on I never called him anything other than Infinite or King again. I felt crazy calling him Alex in the beginning of this journey because of that lesson way back in 2001. In 2002, Alex asked if I would be his celli in a two-man cubicle with a bunk bed. He had the bottom and I had the top. For me that was an honor considering he could have chosen anyone in the unit. His asking me meant he trusted me and I had gained his respect. Respect and trust are everything in prison. We were cellmates for the next three years, which meant day in and day out, good, bad or ugly we were in the trenches together. It was during this time that we transformed our friendship into a brothership.

On so many nights we'd build on different topics and sharpen each other's mental skills. I left Butner in 2005 and got out of prison altogether in 2008. Alex got out a few years later. It wasn't until 2016 that we finally saw each other again, but we kept up with each other's success, often reaching out through Messenger. Each time I would graduate, or he would accomplish something, we would reach out and say "congrats, bro." We would talk occasionally and text often, but it wasn't until Jan. 9, 2016, when he invited me to come hear some spoken word that we saw each other for the first time since 2005. That was a great night because I got to see my bro do what he does best: engage the crowd like no other.

That night I met Alisha for the first time. She was cool but not too friendly. I mean she spoke, but she wasn't the warm, loving sis I know now, LOL. Actually, I thought, *damn, she's mean as hell. She is serious, and not one to play with.* That night I was introduced to people I will always be connected to, though I didn't know it at the time. Fast forward a year or so later. I was in Salisbury and reached out to Alex and told him where I would be. He came where I was and we chopped it up. This was the first time I noticed something was wrong because his fingers were bent in a way that resembled a half-fist. I didn't know how to ask what was wrong, so I simply asked, "Is everything ok?" He told me he had ALS. He briefly mentioned he was doing his research, said something about stem cells and that he was going to do everything he could to beat it. I remember saying to myself *DAMN BRO*. Before I left, he let me know he was always here for me when I was ready to start my business. We said our goodbyes, expressed our mutual love and went on with our lives.

Fast forward six months or more. I was in Salisbury getting tires with my bike bro, and I told him I must stop by and see my bro while I'm here. So, we did. This would be the second time I met Alisha, but this time she was warmer and inviting. I told her then not to hesitate to call me if she needed me. After we left, I couldn't get out of the driveway fast enough before I literally had to stop the truck and break down. I was overwhelmed with emotion and cried like a baby. I was broken. It killed me to see my brother, King, (Alex) in a wheelchair and hooked up to an oxygen machine. My bike bro said, "Man, this dude must really mean a lot to you." I told him, "Bro, you don't even know." I proceeded to tell him that we did five years together in the same unit and were cellmates for three of those years. We helped each other when we had no one else. We grew together. We hurt together. We went to classes together. We walked the track together. We constantly built together. We ate together. We will forever be bonded. He told me he respected me even more now than he did before and we left to head back to the Boro. I would never have imagined what came next: Alex was in the hospital fighting for his life. In my mind I was thinking *what the &%$#* So, I went to see him, and he was hooked up to a bunch of tubes and machines. Alisha was there and she looked beat. I told her to go home and I would watch King. I gave her my keys and that began our two-year journey that would test all of us, teach us and bond us forever.

While I was there, others came in to see Alex, but this one bro came in fresh, dressed like a million bucks. (He was probably wearing real Gucci socks.) This bro was Nick Means. We introduced ourselves and the rest is history. I remember Alex had to be suctioned, and I asked him if he wanted to do it. Nick said, "Nah, I'm good. You look like you got it." By the end of this journey, Nick was doing it all with no problem. Now he's my brother for life. From that day forward, I was there every other day if not every day. Funny story. After Alex woke up and was more alert, I tried to come up with creative ways for him to communicate with us because he couldn't talk at the time. I tried creating ways to exercise his mental strength because I know he loved to build and learn. So, when he finally came around and was able to talk a little, one of the first full sentences we heard him say, barely above a whisper, was "You can leave." Nick, Alisha and I looked at each other and fell out laughing. I told him, "First bro, I'm here to help you. I've been here helping your butt since you were admitted. I'm not going anywhere. You're stuck with me, bro."

That was a funny moment. We had a lot of great times

UNLIKELIEST OF FRIENDSHIPS

Greg Edds

I share these memories, just like most of you, simply as Alex's friend. For a time, Alex and I referred to our relationship as "the unlikeliest of friendships." We were separated by age, race, friendship circles, politics and life experiences—tough odds in today's climate.

I first met Alex at a public event in 2014, at which he was the guest speaker. He openly spoke about his past, talking about his life's choices and their consequences. But then he spoke about the future and hope and how the next positive choice you make can help change your destiny and the destiny of those around and behind you.

Later that week, my son and I were in town and saw Alex outside a local business. I introduced them and told my son how inspiring it was to hear Alex speak earlier that week. I asked Alex if he would briefly relay his inspiring message to my son. Alex turned his body -—and his full attention—to my son and talked to him for ten minutes about making good choices, pursuing his life's passion and the value of being a good man.

I'm certain Alex was busy, but that was a moment he set aside to invest in my son and a moment that neither my son nor I will ever forget. I am grateful for that appointed time together.

Anyone who ever heard Alex speak knows what a wonderful gift he had. He was highly intelligent. He studied people, and he was an astute observer of men.

We all know about the loving commitment he and his wife, Alisha, demonstrated to the youth of our community with their amazing work through Gemstones & Compass Leadership Academy. So many kids have learned about life and life skills from their remarkable work. But Alex was also intimately interested in the role that men play in our community and in their families—and how they related to and supported other men.

In 2015, Alex and I began to meet occasionally to talk about our community and how we could combine efforts to help improve Rowan County. I call those get-togethers "Meetings with Alex…the Chess Player.". One time Alex was talking to me about his love of chess and said, "In the beginning, I didn't do it right because I wasn't looking at the whole board."

To be honest, I wasn't really sure whether he was talking about the game of chess or the game of life. He paused for a moment then said, "Man, look at all of the time we've wasted by not studying the whole board."

We continued strengthening our relationship over time, and the most foundational development we built was the gift of trust. Our time together created trust, trust created friendship, friendship created a mutual love for one another and that love created a deep commitment.

By 2019, our relationship had deepened. As we know, during that time Alex developed ALS and also married the love of his life. But he also began focusing intently on personally mentoring people by pouring his whole heart into them.

Occasionally, I would make a batch of chocolate chip cookies and take some to him, hoping to exchange cookies for some personal time together. I did it out of love for him and a real desire to minister to *him* as a friend with a horrible disease. I was such a rookie! As most of you could predict, it wasn't long before I found that I was the one who was actually being ministered to. But he still loved my cookies!

During our visits, I would always have my phone out and send myself texts with "Alex quotes" attached. He'd throw out so many solid thoughts I often couldn't type them fast enough and would get frustrated with myself for losing some of his wonderful phrasing.

Later, I transcribed my text notes to a Word document. When I completed my transcription, I read back through Alex's words and found myself, with eyes full of tears, thankful that I had chronicled so many of our conversations together. Below are some of my favorite "Alex thoughts."

- *"When I look back on my life, my struggles played a critical role in producing my victories. I wouldn't be who I am without the pain. Even if I had the power to do so, I wouldn't change a thing."*
- *"I have been blessed to travel the road of many unknowns."*
- *"Men, we need to do the right thing because it's the right thing to do."*
- *"As men, it's important to have courage. But it's infinitely more important to have character."*
- *"One thing I've learned about men is, there are role models and there are wrong models."*
- *"I don't see enough living men ministering to other living men."*
- *"Once you get in tune with doing the right thing because it's the right thing to do, at that point, what's right doesn't come FROM you. What's right comes THROUGH you."*
- *"When I learn to look at you as my brother, I learn to look at you as my other self. So, regardless (of) the circumstances, how can I possibly come to hate myself?"*
- *About his mother:" I learned everything about life and love from my mother. I wouldn't trade her for the world."*
- *About Alisha:" She loved me, not only in spite of who I used to be, but for who I had the potential to be. And I love her beyond life for that."*
- *A quote from Alex's doctors:" YOU don't see you, but WE see you. And you will NEVER be able to see the strength that we do. The entire medical staff talks about you often, your strength, and how you just won't give up."*

The last five weeks of Alex's ministry were spent in ICU. There were a few things I could always count on when I went to visit. One, Nick Means would always be there. Two, Alex would always have that award-winning smile on his face. Three, I would always receive a good word of encouragement or wisdom from him. And four, I would always get to meet someone from Alex's past whose life had been wonderfully changed.

Perhaps the most moving introductions I encountered were with people who had served time with Alex in prison. I met folks from Washington D.C., North Carolina, Virginia and many other places I don't even remember. Each one of their stories shared a common theme: "Alex changed *his own life* and then spent the rest of our time together changing mine."

I was honored to meet Alex's friend, Sean, from Raleigh, N.C. Sean said it best, and I'll never forget it. "Everything I am I owe to Alex. Because of how he helped me change my life, I now spend every waking moment trying to rebuild the very community that I spent my whole life trying to destroy." What a legacy!

Alisha was kind enough to allow my wife and I to spend some time with Alex the night he passed away. He was alert and, as always, smiling. We prayed with him. We cried with him. We celebrated with him. We sang a hymn with him.

Alisha, thank you for sharing Alex with so many of us and for your unwavering, loving support of your husband. Alex's life is a clear, wonderful picture of God's grace, forgiveness, mercy and redemption.

Alex fully believed that his struggles were a beautiful, priceless bridge to the ministry that he loved so much. "When I look back on my life," he said, "my struggles played a critical role in producing my victories. I wouldn't be who I am without the pain. Even if I had the power to do so, I wouldn't change a thing."

Men, if Alex were standing here today, he'd tell you to be a man of good character. Minister to other living men. Be a ROLE model, and not a WRONG model. Remember that doing what's right doesn't come FROM you, but it comes THROUGH you. Do the right thing, because it's the right thing to do. Love your mama. Love your wife. Don't waste precious time…study the whole board. Give your very best. No regrets. Don't ever give up.

Alex was my friend and I loved him and our time together. I thank God for his life and his influence over me, and you and countless others. I reminded him often that his positive influence would be felt for generations.

When I think back on the phrase "unlikely friendship," it sounds a little offensive to me today. It was a friendship that taught both of us a tremendous amount. It's an example of a friendship that should, and needs, to become a common story in this community and, quite frankly, around our nation.

What is *your* life's story? Is it one of grace? Mercy? Forgiveness? Hope? Do you have your own personal redemption story? You've seen a miracle, close up, clearly modeled in the remarkable life of a man that we love and honor.

I hope that the way he lived his life encourages each of us to be better men, better women, better sisters and brothers, better husbands and wives and better friends.

As we left Alex's hospital room for the last time, I removed his cap, kissed him on the top of his head and said "I'll see you later." He smiled that "Alex smile" and replied, "I'll see you later."

I thank God for the hope that Alex had within him that gives each of us the confidence to say, "We'll see you later."

A MOTHER'S HEART

Margaret Clark Robinson

When the letter came in the mail, I don't know what made me open it. Alex, Shawn, Hen and I were candid with one another, but after I heard the diagnosis I Googled it. ALS: Fatal. No cure. Three to five years to live. It felt as if my head swelled into a balloon, as though I was suddenly trapped inside a vacuum. I left the house and walked in the woods of my garden. I came back inside Googled ALS again, desperately hoping my eyes had been playing tricks on me the first time. Then I cried. And I screamed. And I cried some more. I cried out to God, asking Him to please spare my son. I asked God why. I was upset and mad with Him. Then I asked Him why again. I kicked, stomped and cried until my stomach hurt. I called Shawn and Hen.

Out of the blue, it seemed Alex and Alisha arrived. I took him to the bedroom and asked why he didn't fully explain to me what was going on, why he didn't tell me about this illness that was making him limp. He looked at me and said, "We will get through this." I said, "But it's going to kill you." Then we all discussed it.

His wish was to be able to tell the world, so I stood back. I still didn't know all about ALS, but I knew enough to know that it wasn't anything good. All I wanted was for him to be home and for my family to be together.

Over the days as his disease progressed, the nurse would call to ask how many times he'd fallen. Since he didn't live with me, I didn't know. So when we talked on the phone, I'd ask whether he was having that problem yet? He replied no, not yet. Then I placed my focus more on him, visiting at his home more frequently and encouraging our immediate family to do the same.

Then, one day I saw him fall. It was as if I got kicked in the stomach. It felt like' I was watching a horror movie as a monster consumed my son's body and there was nothing I could do to stop it. Don't get me wrong. I know and believe in God, but I was still upset with Him, my soul was uneasy and my spirit was weak. I cried everyday as I still do.

When I asked my son how he handled having ALS, he told me he handled it as he thought Jesus would.

One day I was crying and fussing, still questioning what I had done for my son to receive such a horrible diagnosis. Afterwards, I felt calm. I could hear my mother telling me I shouldn't question God, so I asked for forgiveness and asked for His guidance and strength.

Just know I would have traded places with my son in a heartbeat were that possible. I thank God that through all of this he had the best, greatest, most compassionate and loving wife. He was also blessed with friends and family that showered him with all of the love they could give. Some people are afraid to love, but I say let it flow. We have to be brave and bold to get things done, and when you truly love, can't is not an option. Also, when you're going through, you learn who really has your back and who doesn't.

To tell the truth, a couple of times when someone asked me how Alex was doing, I told them to go see for themselves. Like I said, I learned something about my people as my son fought for his life.

Cancer is bad but ALS is a true monster. It takes a body all the way out. My baby left because he knew that after his voice left him, he would be "locked in." ALS is an unnatural disease. I pray that one-day no one will have to endure its unforgiving sting—one that all the love and prayers can't take away.

"I'm crying everyone's tears. And there inside the private war I died the night before. And all of these remnants of joy and disaster. What am I supposed to do? I want to cook you a soup that warms your soul. But nothing would change, nothing would change at all. It's just a day that brings it all about. Just another day and nothing's any good. (Sade).

I thank God for my husband, Garry. When I tell him about how I feel, he understands. When I think about my "KIDD,", = my super "KIDD" and how he fought, how he accepted his fate and realized he had fought the good fight, I smile warmly. He has shown how he was favored, even in death.

God allowed my son to stay on this earth long enough to give his last speech to the children. He kept COVID-19 away from Alex and allowed him to leave all of his worldly words here. Then he sent his grandmother, "Mama Short," to get him.

I simply cannot say enough about his wife, Alisha, or about how grateful I am for her. I love her for how she loved and cared for my son. I also don't have adequate or enough words to thank his friends Nick, Suave, Nico, Timothy Bates and Anthony. Alex was a beautiful soul, one who always gave more than he was given. When I close my eyes at night or even when I'm wide awake during the day, I always see him smiling. I see my little one anxious for his first ride on the school bus in his little red ball cap. I hear him telling me he wants us to go catch dragonflies. I see him being the big brother, my super "KIDD." Lord knows I miss him so much!

6

Summer Breeze

SACRIFICES

Alex and I shared what we needed to with those in our circle. The community saw what we decided to share, which was everlasting love and strength.

I'd like to pose a question. What are you willing to sacrifice so that others may have what they need? Be it your spouse, your children or your close friends? What, exactly, are you willing to sacrifice for them?

Before Alex and I got married, we became business owners and co-founders of a nonprofit organization. He invested in my dream financially before we even thought about saying "I Do." He believed in my dreams and was willing to help me accomplish them no matter what.

When I said "I Do" to Alex, I was willing to sacrifice it all no matter what because I knew within my heart Alex was heaven-sent and God had prepared and equipped me for this journey. Just a few weeks into our "honeymoon phase," our entire lives changed, we were dealing with a serious health crisis as Alex's ALS was finally staring us smack in the face. I had to give it all up—I put working and our businesses, into which we invested money and time, on the back burner. I put my sorority sisters on hold and attended meetings and functions only when we had a nurse available. I even had to put going to church on hold –so that my husband could receive the best quality of life possible.

Spending quality time with our daughter, sons and grandchildren was not the easiest thing to do and doing many of the things to which we'd grown accustomed. Our children never complained, but I'm quite sure a little quality time outside of the hospital would've been appreciated. Alex was immobile most of the time, so picking up and going places wasn't easy.

God blessed me with the man I needed, wanted and prayed for, and regardless of what I had to give up for him to live and have a decent quality of life, I was willing to do just that. The part of the vows that says in sickness and in health, for better and for worse is real.

Was it easy? Absolutely not. Was it worth it? No question. This season of sacrifice in which we found ourselves forced a career change for me. I hung up my CEO hat and donned a nurse's hat. In fact, I wore many hats while caring for Alex: Nurse Practitioner, Respiratory Therapist and, sometimes, Physician with limited experience. I had to shift some things around and get my mind in the right frame to provide the level of care Alex needed.

We both prided ourselves on being adept at research, so when Alex was diagnosed with ALS, we became the Google King and Queen. We did our homework and familiarized ourselves with relevant terminology to ensure we were never in the dark when the doctors spoke to us about Alex's status. Suffice it to say, we made it our business to stay ahead of the curve.

I sacrificed a few things, but so did Alex. He put himself in danger by continuing to attend Dinner and Dialogue meetings with COMPASS (for men and boys), which usually landed him in the hospital within forty-eight hours afterwards. Attending community functions so he could voice his opinion regarding matters of his heart always caused additional stress on his body afterwards. Celebrating his life with a surprise party with family and friends resulted in a hospital stay days later. Although he could have easily said no, he was willing to risk his health for the love of people and community.

It's not always easy to make sacrifices for those you love, even though you love them. Nonetheless, together Alex and I were willing to make many sacrifices not only for each other but for others also.

I began working at age sixteen and formed a solid work ethic, eventually becoming accustomed to a certain lifestyle after college. So did Alex. We never went without the basic necessities and were even able to acquire some luxuries on the side. We both had experienced owning nice cars and living in comfortable homes. Designer this and designer that. But when ALS hit, none of that mattered. Our monetary and luxury habits changed once we got married, we went from being business owners to living on a very tight, fixed income, living within our means. We found it necessary to do whatever we had to for Alex to receive the medical care he needed to live as comfortably as possible.

One thing I can say is little became much when we placed it in God's hands. We may not have had luxurious items or lived as large as before, but we were oh so rich in love. We never complained about not having money with which to do this and that because God always provided for us by sending someone our way to bless us.

IMPACT

I never witnessed what one man can have on other men until Alex's ALS progression became worse. His walking days had ended and he relied heavily on wheelchair.

As word got out about Alex being hospitalized, his room would be surrounded with men coming to pray with and encourage him—only to receive the same in return. I remember several of those occasions. Once, his friend Greg told him he sometimes felt selfish because he'd come to lift Alex's spirits and encourage him but would leave with more that he gave. Another gentleman found out Alex was at Moses Cone, came unannounced and said he was contemplating suicide and needed so see Alex to regain his strength. One told Alex that after following his journey, he began praying on his knees again because he wanted God to reverse his condition.

Alex asked me to get in touch with a local pastor and ask him to come pray for him. During their first face-to-face encounter, Alex began ministering to him. The pastor in turn ministered to Alex by telling him, "Alex, you have done more on your back than most men have done on their feet."

I have seen grown men shed some big tears because of the knowledge and wisdom Alex shared with them. He had a way of reaching into those four areas described in Joharis Window: open, blind, hidden and unknown. Part of his purpose was his men's ministry, and he fulfilled every part of it on earth. He listened to the cares and concerns that boys and men had, allowing them to get it all out. Then he assisted them in finding ways to be better than they were. I found out that sometimes people gain strength from what others are challenged by.

The impact Alex made on so many has been lasting. To hear others, tell stories about who he was to them makes me even more thankful for being his chosen one.

I'm grateful to be able to share two stories from women in our community:

GOOD ENOUGH

Talita McCain

Alex Clark always made me feel like I was "good enough" when others tried to make me question it. He always let me know that the works I tried to do in the community did not go unnoticed. I remember he would call to see how things were going with the first business Angie and I started. He'd always offer advice, ideas, and most importantly, encouragement and support. I remember him always telling me that I WAS extraordinary and to "KEEP BEING EXTRAORDINARY." Every time I left his presence, I thought about all the lives he's touched and his love for youth. Duke was the change he wanted to see in the world! He was so knowledgeable, positive, purpose-driven and strong... His life and legacy are nothing less than EXTRAORDINARY!!!

RESILIENCY

Ms. Renoda Burns

Alex is a true example of resiliency! Way before ALS started to take a toll on his body, he was an up-lifter, encourager and motivator! ALS didn't stop him! He always had a gem or nugget of wisdom for you to take and ponder when you departed.

Even during the days when he struggled the most, when it took a lot for him to even speak, he used those breaths to inspire us to keep on keeping on! I know he had rough days, but somehow he always found a way to smile, sing and brighten our days!

The youth were his PASSION and his wife and family were his HEART! So in essence, he lives on through the many lives he's impacted! Alex, ALL the work you've done is not in vain!!

7

Earthquake

Last 21 Days

WHEN IT HURTS TO LIVE

The first time I heard those words leave Alex's mouth was after returning home from a rather long hospital stay. We were watching TV and out of the blue he started getting emotional and had me call his parents, siblings and our village.

Once everyone arrived, Alex told us with tears in his eyes that he felt as if he was running out of time. "I'm not saying I'm leaving tomorrow or next week, but I don't have long," he said. "We all know the inevitable is going to take place." As much as I, his wife, knew there was no cure for ALS and that he'd been diagnosed with the terminal illness, the last thing I wanted to hear was something like this. By no means did I feel as though Alex was giving up. Instead, he was just preparing us for what he felt in his spirit.

We listened attentively to what he had to say. Some cried, some fought back tears and others were consoling. I silently called on Jesus! Lord, while you are preparing him, please prepare my heart.

Alex's words, "when it hurts to live, it ain't living," made me see things through a different lens. He tried so hard to be strong for those close and dear to his heart, and he did an amazing job concealing from us how he really felt deep down inside.

Nonetheless, there comes a time in everyone's life when you have to be transparent, open and honest with those you love. For Alex the time had come. When he said those words, it hurt to the deepest parts of my core. My husband. Mr. Wonderful. My Sympathetic Soul was hurting emotionally, spiritually and physically and life was beginning not to be worth living.

"A machine is breathing for me daily," he said. "I have a hole in my throat and used to have a tube in my stomach. I can't scratch my head when it itches. I can't feed myself, dress myself or even stand on my own two feet. That's not living, and it hurts." Even though I tried my best to substitute for his hands and his feet, it hurt me just as much—not only because he was my husband but because he was a man who was feeling less than. He could provide for his household financially but couldn't assist me with basic household duties. Even when it hurt and as much as it did, he still lived a life of purpose.

EXTENDED STAY

Who would've thought we'd be spending another holiday in the hospital? After entertaining family during Christmas, here we are again calling 911 because Alex is having difficulty breathing while on five liters of oxygen. Although he was supposed to have been admitted simply for overnight observation, he spiked a 103-degree temperature, indicating an infection.

I was so hoping to bring in 2020 in our home, but it wasn't meant to be. On New Year's Eve, our plan was to make a vision board and set goals for the upcoming year. I purchased all of the supplies only for them to go unused due to both of us falling asleep before the New Year arrived.

Over in the morning, we looked into each other's eyes, which were filled with thankfulness for another chance to live, love and laugh. Despite what the doctors said, we made it to 2020. With a collapsed lung and stable vitals, Alex was discharged and told he could safely return home with a Midline IV Catheter and a fourteen-day supply of antibiotics.

After being home for a few days, we found ourselves right back where we started. My aunt and uncle had a dual retirement party, and although the weather was not as favorable as we'd hoped, Alex was determined to attend their celebration. I told him several times that going was not the best idea because of the way his body was already starting to feel, but he was in a stubborn, determined mood so we got ourselves together and joined the family. The entire time we were there, Alex looked so uncomfortable. I knew something wasn't right. During dinner he didn't want anything to eat, and we found ourselves going back and forth to the bathroom more than usual. An hour in, I asked him if he was ready to go home and he said "No, not home. To the hospital. I knew then something was definitely wrong.

When we were several blocks away from the hospital, Alex told me to call the ER and tell them to have help at the door. Once we pulled up, I got out and ran in the hospital screaming for help. By this time, Alex was acting the same way he did when he experienced respiratory failure. The ER doctor ordered a series of tests, including another CT scan. This time the test revealed a blood clot in Alex's lung.

Wait a minute. We were just here two weeks ago and his tests were negative. Now he has a blood clot in his lung? How in the world did that happen so quickly? This is the same lung that collapsed during the last visit.

In addition, Alex was not responding the way he generally did. He was constantly urinating and losing control of his bodily functions. Usually he was good about telling me or his nurses when he had to use the bathroom, and he complained if his clothing became soiled. But this time he said nothing.

The nurses we always had in the Critical Care Unit (CCU) were surprised we were back so soon. They are always excited to see us, but not under those circumstances.

It didn't take them long to pick up on the fact that this time something was definitely wrong and different. They catered to Alex a little more and offered additional support to me. One offered prayer and others went out of their way to drop in, even when Alex was not their patient.

One of the nurses went above and beyond to plan a hospital date for us. Alex had made such an impression on the nurses, doctors and even the kitchen staff because his heart and love for people were just as infectious as his smile.

2-YEAR ANNIVERSARY

Oh, what a night! I literally watched Alex's heart rate go from the low 70s to 197 with a blood pressure of 253 over 136. His oxygen rate had dropped to 76. I heard a nurse say, "If we don't give him a dose of ******, he's going to code."

The next day, Alex made his last Facebook live video. I could tell he was tired, but he looked at me with this big smile on his face.

During the video, I asked him how he was feeling. His response was, "I am exhausted, but I am still here. It could've been over last night, but God saw me through, so whatever you decide to do with your life, do something great with it.... I Love You." Despite what he was going through, he still had a positive message for the people watching

Fifteen minutes after I posted the video, Alex's heart rate and blood pressure shot up again. He was staring at me and I couldn't do anything but cry. I was beyond helpless as I watched every nurse and doctor in the unit rush to his room. Once they pulled the pads out to shock him, I lost it. I was asking God to give him more time. Not to take him like this. I ran out of his room and called family and our village. I didn't know if Alex was alive or not now. I was scared, confused and a total wreck.

Our second anniversary was around the corner, and although we didn't want to spend it in the hospital, my prayer to God was to please allow Alex to be here with me when it came. God granted my prayer, and the hospital staff, aware of our anniversary, made it very memorable for us. We lived, we loved and we laughed. We celebrated another year of happiness regardless of where we were physically. As always, we ended our night with a prayer, by telling each other "I love you" and by telling God thank you.

PROMISES

During one of my school visits, I was approached by a high school teacher who had recently been informed about Alex having ALS. Her class was reading "Tuesdays with Morrie," a book about a man who visited a college professor who was diagnosed with and later died from ALS. She asked whether Alex would be willing to talk to her class about his ALS journey, and without hesitation he agreed. We had set a date, put a plan in motion and here came another hospital visit.

Two days before Alex was promised to speak, he woke up very emotional. He said, "I made a promise to the kids. What are we going to do to make this happen?" I made a visit to the school, talked to Principal Brown and told him about our situation. He said, "Don't worry. I will take care of it." Before I knew it, we were on a test ZOOM call preparing for the next day.

The kids assembled in the auditorium, and Alex was comfortable in his hospital bed with a computer in front of him. He was ready to do what he did best: have an open dialogue with youth.

Alex opened by telling his story, which included the symptoms he started having, his diagnosis and how he was feeling about the entire situation. He told them that ALS began as a fight, became a battle and then an all-out war. He allowed the students to ask questions. One student asked whether he was afraid of death. Alex responded with a smile on his face. "Well, that is inevitable. Nobody gets out alive. However, I do love living, but I know one day it will happen because of ALS."

I shared the video on Facebook, and before we knew it word had spread around the hospital about it. His doctors and nurses were so amazed at the strength he was able to find, for one, but also over the impact he was still continuing to make.

Later that afternoon, the teacher brought thirty handmade cards to Alex from the students. The cards were taped on the walls for everyone to see and as a special reminder to him of the lives he was still touching—even from his hospital bed. Those who entered his room stood in amazement when they saw the handmade cards from high school students.

We were later told that the students were beyond grateful for their encounter with Alex. Not only did they enjoy talking to him; they were moved by the fact that he kept his promise.

WAR

I concealed Alex's last hospital stay from a lot of family and friends because by then things were just different and he needed his rest.

By now, Alex had several blood clots in his lung. He had three bronchoscopies to drain the excess fluid from his lung, and his body was taking a beating. He was constantly in pain, which was very abnormal. Those for whom he asked came in with heavy hearts because they could not stand to see him the way he was.

His inability to talk as loud as before was heartbreaking. He had to stop continuously to take a deep breath just to share his thoughts. Alex was a talker, so trust me, he had plenty to say and his guests were patient because they wanted to hear what he had to say.

One day out of the blue, I asked Alex to describe to me how he was feeling. Below are his words:

"One day it's' a fight, a battle, a war. I'm at war every single day. It's not about the strides. It's about millimeters, the centimeter, half inches. With what I'm dealing with the smallest measurements matter most.

The psychological impact from having a hole in my throat is indescribable. Unless you have one, you will never understand.

To be told that you have pneumonia, to take every antibiotic prescribed for a certain number of days only to be told that you still have it after you've finished the prescription, takes a serious toll on you.

To have a bronchoscopy one day, then to have fluid and mucus build up a few days later takes a serious toll on your body." Needless to say, Alex didn't mince words but instead gave it to me straight. Of course I expected no less.

TRANSITIONING

One night when I was so drained and exhausted from being at the hospital, Nick happened to come by. Immediately he said, "Sis, get some rest. I'll be here for a while." Nick must have left after seeing both Alex and I were sleeping. The next thing I knew, I awakened to hear Alex fussing with some nurses. "She's over there asleep," I heard him say. "I've been calling her for minutes now. I'm wet and need to be moved and changed."

His eyes were filled with anger and disappointment.

I felt horrible because I didn›t hear him calling my name. I was so tired… Yet I had never seen Alex so mad…

The more I apologized, the angrier he became. While we were dating and thus far throughout our marriage, Alex had never looked at me that way. He was uncomfortable, wet, disappointed and angry.

After getting changed and rearranged, he asked Jamie, the Nurse Practitioner to take down all of the cards the students had made for him, saying he didn't want this toxic environment to rub off on the kids. It was then when I knew he was fading away and something was terribly wrong.

The next day Nick and Alex's mom came to the hospital to calm him down, but he didn't remember what had happened the night before or why he was so mad and angry towards me. He looked at me with tears in his eyes and said he would never do anything to hurt me, but the pain I felt from the toll ALS was taking on my husband told my mind and heart something different.

This horrific disease was attacking the most beautiful parts of him—his heart, mind and soul.—and I, out of all people, bore witness to it.

I needed a breather and decided to take a walk. On my way to the cafeteria, I ran into one of Alex's doctors. He asked if he could talk to me privately about Alex's condition. As I agreed to speak with him, he began to share that ALS was progressing and Alex was starting to transition. He knew about the attacks, the anger and Alex being mean to me. He told me Alex's behavior had absolutely nothing to do with me. "Alex knows that his days are limited, and you are the closest person to him that he›s afraid of leaving," his doctor said. "It's like being in a bad relationship and someone has to break up with the other person before it gets worse."

I saw his mouth moving, but this college-educated woman was having a hard time comprehending. "Let me try this again," I said to the doctor. "Did you say my husband, my Alex, my sympathetic soul, my best friend, my prayer partner, my biggest fan and supporter is dying and has limited days to live?

"Unfortunately yes, that's what I'm saying," he replied with six words that for Alex and me were life-changing.

Alex confided in his doctor more and more while trying to protect my heart by not telling me directly what was going on with him.

After leaving the hospital to go home to regroup, I received a call while in the shower having my morning cry. The doctor on the other end of the line mentioned that Alex wanted to receive visits from several people, including Terrance. Terrance is Alex's son. Problem is he passed away at age 11 ½ twenty years ago after losing his battle with leukemia.

When the doctor said Terrance's name, I couldn't believe my ears and asked her to repeat it. I also asked if she was sure Alex had said Terrance. Her reply was, "Yes, I wrote it down to be sure and asked him twice as well."

Now, I must say that Terrance is also the name of the husband of my girlfriend, Nicole, so I asked her to bring him to the hospital to see if Alex reacted in a certain way. When they arrived, there wasn't anything out of the ordinary about their interaction.

I never asked Alex to explain exactly *which* Terrance he was referencing when he told his doctor he wanted to see Terrance. I didn't "go there" with Alex because I really didn't want to accept the fact that he could actually be transitioning and asking for his deceased son. It's been said by many that when people start to transition not only do they see people who've passed away; they also start asking for them and talking about them as well. Even though several signs were staring me smack in the face, neither my heart—nor my mind—was able to accept what was really going on.

I struggled for days and finally built up the strength to have a heart-to-heart conversation with Alex. One thing he asked me was not to let him suffer. For days I watched him being poked and prodded. I watched him asking for pain meds and meds for anxiety, at one point he wouldn't even take Tylenol.

While sharing our hearts with each other, I asked him if we could just go home and spend his final days there. With tears in both of our eyes, he grabbed my hand and said "Queen, I don't want to bring death in our home. Although he was very certain that he was getting closer and closer to the end, I just wanted us to go home. He on the other hand, wanted to spare me the additional hurt and pain and wanted our home to be the way we left it before going to the retirement party- peaceful.

I finally allowed myself to come to terms with telling him it's OK! He was at peace but I was so far from it. The same way I gave the doctors permission to put him on life support, I was giving my husband permission to leave me. Those were the two hardest decisions I've ever made in my life. Alex told me he'd been waiting for me to say those words so he could be at peace. "Queen, you did everything right," he said. "You honored and protected the vows you made to me, but it's time for me to go. I'm tired of wrestling with God."

For days afterwards, I was on pins and needles, trying to wrap my mind around how I was going to manage without the love of my life. The more I tried displaying strength, the more my world started caving in. We had just celebrated our second year of marriage. We had just celebrated Valentine's Day. Next would be the Celebration of his Life and Legacy.

LIVING ON EMPTY

I've made no secret of the fact that I cried out to God numerous times, asking Him why Alex was afflicted with ALS. I've also been clear that God never answered me. That's right. No matter how many times I questioned Him...crickets.

The Bible tells us in Matthew 7:7, "Ask, and it will be given to you; seek, and you will find; knock, and it will be opened to you." Those of you who know Jesse and Minnie Byrd know they were all about The Lord and their family. So you know that means I was raised in the church. Which means, of course, that I grew up hearing "Ask and it shall be given. Seek and ye shall find." So you already know what I'm about to say next. Why on earth in my darkest hours, in my lowest points, in my most critical time of need, was God forsaking me? Why wasn't He answering me? Why was he just leaving me out there, blowing in the wind, like a lost child who can't find his way home?

As the days turned to weeks and the weeks turned to months, I continued feeling as though God had abandoned me. I'd hear people say they were praying for Alex and me, and I'd think to myself, *I hope God answers you because he sho nuff hasn't answered me.*

We've all had times in our lives when we felt like nobody cared. Like we were all alone. Like it was us against the world. At times during Alex's illness, that is exactly how I felt. To be sure, there were plenty of friends and relatives who were there for me and for Alex, but nonetheless, that is how I felt at times. Maybe I felt that way during my private pity parties. Dunno. But, like I said, that's how I felt at times. And not getting answers from God only worsened matters for me. Now don't get me wrong. I continued believing in God and praising Him and going to church. I never lost faith in God. I just didn't understand why He was ignoring me.

I should say at this point that whenever things got really bad with Alex, whenever it appeared as though this might be the moment when he slips away, I always cried out to God. And, every time except, well, you know…God allowed Alex to live to see another day. So now that I think about it, God *was* answering me. I guess it's more accurate to say He wasn't answering me the way I thought he should answer me. You know how sometimes people say God gave them a sign? I guess that's what I was looking for. I wanted a clear sign, just as plain as the nose on my face, from God about how I was supposed to handle Alex's illness, about what I was supposed to do. Like the time I asked his mother whether I should put him on the ventilator and she told me she would support whatever decision I made. God bless her heart, but even she didn't give me a clear-cut answer. Instead, she left it up to me to decide. She put that monumental decision in my hands. True, I was Alex's wife at the time, so legally the decision was mine to make, but I guess I thought Alex's mother would give me her opinion on what I should do instead of just leaving it all up to me. Leaving it up to me. Just like God was doing.

In case you're wondering, I wasn't angry at God. Not at all. I just simply didn't understand; couldn't understand why He wasn't answering me. Why he was leaving me out to wing it on my own. I'm an educated woman, but the way God was treating me just didn't make sense to me. It was like comparing oranges and apples—no matter how I sliced it.

Over time I kind of stopped wondering why God wasn't answering me. Instead, I channeled my energy into caring for Alex and doing my absolute best to keep him encouraged and in good spirits. Don't misconstrue what I'm saying here. I always did my best taking care of Alex, but once I let go of my "issue" with God, it seemed I was able to exhale a little more as I took care of my precious Alex, the love of my life.

DYING EMPTY

The day before Alex passed away, he told me that he still had some wisdom and knowledge to share with others. His words were, "Queen, when I die, I want to leave here empty." There are self-made millionaires in the cemetery who left here full of wisdom and ideas that they didn't' share. I don't want to leave here like that.

Everyone who came in his hospital room received some sort of encouragement from Alex that day. His voice was beginning to fade in and out, but that didn't stop him from sharing what was on his heart and mind.

I had placed a NO VISITORS sign on the door, and only those who had made prior arrangements were allowed to visit. Matt was standing in the hallway looking in the closed door. I invited him to come in to visit Alex. He came in, grabbed Alex's hand and thanked him for the many contributions he'd made to the community. With tears in his eyes, Alex smiled and poured into Matt, thanking him for the generous way he blessed him and wishing blessings upon his businesses. As we all stood there in amazement, fighting back tears, I understood what Alex meant by dying empty.

He released every ounce of love, hope, joy and peace that resided in him. He emptied out himself. He died empty.

Alex passed away on February 22, 2020, surrounded by his family, close friends and amazing nurses Jamie, Summer, Beverly and Shelly --all of whom he handpicked for this day. As time grew near, with my hand in his, we never said goodbye. The only words we were able to utter were "Thank You" and "I Love You."

GOD ANSWERED

The day after we lost Alex, you'll never guess what happened. I *finally* heard from God. Now, I could have been angry at God for taking so long. I could have just stood SMH (shaking my head) over the irony of His timing. Or, I could have lashed out at anyone and everyone around me. But I did none of that. Instead, I listened to God's answer, which was as clear as a just-washed window on a bright, sunny day and hit me— in a good way—like a ton of bricks.

God told me He didn't answer when I cried out to Him with questions because, in those moments, it was more important that I keep my focus on WHAT Alex was dealing with rather than WHY he was dealing with it. God also told me that He put Alex and me together because He knew that I would dutifully handle the responsibilities—all of the enormous, gut-wrenching responsibilities—that were par for the course when caring for someone in Alex's condition. God told me He knew I had what it takes to properly care for Alex without losing every fiber of me in the process. God told me He knew I had the mental fortitude to handle caring for Alex knowing all the while that one day he would no longer need my care. That one day he would be with Him. God told me that I had done an excellent job of caring for Alex and that He was proud of me. Then, God reminded me of Proverbs 18:22, "He who finds a wife finds a good thing, And obtains favor from the Lord." Suddenly, it was like I'd had an epiphany. God knew Alex was going to go through his ALS battle. And God knew Alex needed someone on whom he could trust to care for him, have his back and hold his hand throughout the battle. And for that monumental task, God chose me. Now, a day after Alex waved the white flag of surrender, a day after he was finally able to truly rest, God was giving me more answers than I ever imagined. On this day, God was letting me know that I took care of His child, Alex, the proper way. God was smiling at me on this day, and, even through my heartache and tears, I was able to smile back as I realized the magnitude of what He was saying to me. Deuteronomy 31:6 says, "Be strong and courageous. Do not be afraid or terrified because of them, for the Lord your God goes with you; He will never leave you nor forsake you."

Just like I did not forsake Alex, not even for one minute, God did not forsake me.

Instead, He gave me the strength I needed to get through the rough spots. He gave me the ability to keep keeping on even when my legs grew weary and my eyes were teary. Most importantly, He gave me the strength I needed to be what Alex needed me to be, and he told me unequivocally that my assignment was LOVE.

8

Rainbow

HE LIVED

Some of us have been asked the question, are you existing or are you living.

Are you existing by doing only what is necessary to stay alive? Or are you embracing every moment as it comes, while savoring every moment of your existence for what it is? Are you waking up every morning with purpose, inspired to empower and help others? Are you chasing and fulfilling your dreams and doing whatever it takes to obtain them?

From what I observed, Alex didn't just live. He lived a purpose-driven life with expectations of making a difference in the lives of others.

He became the change he wanted to see by uplifting both men and women during times of discouragement. He did this by mentoring children on a weekly basis with Gemstones and COMPASS Leadership Academy. Moreover, he poured and opened his heart to men and boys while having Dinner and Dialogue with them, discussing life, male issues, community and current events.

"Life's most persistent and urgent question is what are you doing for others?" Dr. Martin Luther King, Jr.

Alex was a leader, a servant, youth advocate and community activist. His daily objective was to make each moment count by including those who wanted to make a difference, who were open to being a catalyst for change and who, like him, were not afraid of becoming the change they desired to see in the world.

Alex didn't just exist. He lived life with purpose. So, now that you've read this book, I have one question for you. Are you existing or are you living?

HE FOUND HIS PURPOSE

Words from Alex Clark

I found my purpose before it ended. Some people never find their purpose and live a meaningless life to which they try to give meaning. I can honestly say all of the things I went through helped me find my purpose, and when the elders confirmed it by putting their stamp on it, I felt like I must be doing the right thing and I had to believe it.

Peace and Blessings

9

Melanated Genius

Before Alex and I got married, he had been secretly putting another MASTER PLAN in place. I had seen him in the "lab" designing images with the words MELANATED GENIUS on it. When I asked what it was, he said he would share in due time.

The next thing I knew, mail was arriving from the United States Patent and Trademark Office. So now the "crazy lady" as he once called me had raised eyebrows and many questions. What is this and what are you doing this time?

Months later, he came in with a box of T-shirts with the image he designed on them. This signature, black T-shirt had MELANATED GENIUS -The REVOLUTION BEGINS IN THE MIND with a red and green fist on it. Leave it to Alex to come up with and create something as such.

Once he showed it to family and friends, they were willing to purchase it and lend support, especially once they understood the meaning behind it.

In his own words, Alex posted the meaning of MELANANTED GENIUS on Facebook for the world to understand.

Peace and Blessings, FAMILY!

As of late, people have been inquiring about MELANATED GENIUS™, as well as where the concept derived from. The inspiration for MELANATED GENIUS™ derived from the innumerable contributions that our Ancestors made to civilization, known and unknown. This is simply my way of paying homage and striving to continue the great work they started for the benefit of humanity.

At MELANATED GENIUS™ we highlight the accomplishments of MELANATED PEOPLE unapologetically. This doesn't mean we don't acknowledge the contributions of others. However, our primary focus is to reintroduce our people to their GREATNESS, as well as what has been strategically kept from us through intentional concealment. Studying the works of intellectual giants such as: Cheik Anta Diop, Theophile Obenga, Dr. Yosef Ben-Jochanan, Dr. John Henricke Clarke, J.A. Rogers, Chancellor Williams, George G.M. James, Ivan Van Sertima, Dr. Frances CressWelsing, Marcus Mosiah Garvey, Ra Un

Nefer Amen, Dr. Phil Valentine, Professor James Smalls, Dr. Leonard Jeffries, The Father, Noble Drew Ali, Elijah Muhammad, Master Fard Muhammad, Dr. Amos Wilson, Dr. Claud Anderson, Ashra Kwesi, and others, gave me a totally different perspective on what it means to tap into my MELANATED GENIUS™, which could be done only by getting to know myself holistically (Strengths and weaknesses.) Whether you know these EXTRAORDINARY scholars or not, we are indebted to them for their courage to challenge a system that did everything it could to suppress and hide the contributions and MELANATED GENIUS™ of our Ancestors. Of course, the list goes on and on.

It's been said that signs and symbols are for the conscious mind, and due to systematic and institutional theft, the signs and symbols that were once used to raise our spiritual vibrations by our Ancestors have been co-opted, which in turn, causes us to normalize functioning on the level of inferior beings.

We're much more than we've been seduced and hypnotized into believing; but have no fear, because the MELANATED GENIUS™ that resides within your spiritual DNA is waiting to be activated to grant your wishes. We were taught religion; however, WE were born a MELANATED GENIUS™. Get to know YOURSELF! Keep being PHENOMENAL!

#MelanatedGENIUS™

QUOTES

By ALex Clark

- The MASTER had a PLAN and I had a PLAN. I'm going to follow the MASTER"S PLAN.
- God made a CHESS move for me. My mind is clear. I'm HAPPY.
- Being at PEACE came with a real fight!
- Salvation is personal. There is nothing anyone can do to put a person where they will spend eternity.
- Sometimes we have to take our light into other people's darkness even when they don't know they are dark.
- Emotions are good servants but poor masters.
- With change we tend to focus on what we have to give up vs what we have to gain.
- The biggest enemy is the inner me!
- When we are so angry, we look for something or someone to take it out on.
- I have the freedom to do what I want to do but I do not have the right to violate you.
- We live by our senses. We want it because it looks good, smells good, taste good and feels good. But we must ask ourselves, is it good?
- Knowledge doesn't belong to anyone. We must all seek it and share it with others.
- Learn what you can. Share what you can. While you can because if you don't share your talents then you waste them and you've wasted your energy.
- The more conscious of self you are, the more at peace you are because you are not looking for an enemy.

- ❖ When people feel they no longer have any use of you they feel like they can treat you like trash but you have to refuse to be thrown in the garbage can".
- ❖ Sometimes God will burn bridges for you so you wont have to cross them.
- ❖ Whatever you choose to do with your life, do something great with it.

JEWELS OF THE DAY

By Alex Clark

11/5/14
You may not make a difference in everybody's life, but know for certain that your presence, support, encouraging words, insight, and assistance makes a BIG DIFFERENCE in SOMEONE'S LIFE. Have a Wonderful day! Peace and Blessings...

3/22/ 2016
SOMETIMES YOU HAVE TO BE SELFISH WITH YOUR TIME. UNDERSTAND THE DIFFERENCE BETWEEN SPENDING IT AND INVESTING IT. ALWAYS REMEMBER, YOU CAN NEVER GET YOUR TIME BACK, SO BE MINDFUL OF WHO AND WHAT YOU INVEST IT IN. #TimeCantBeRecycled

10/6/16
STOP REPLAYING YOUR FAILURE FOOTAGE; BY NOW YOU SHOULD BE TIRED OF WATCHING THOSE RE-RUNS. (CHANGE THE CHANNEL).

DO YOURSELF A FAVOR AND CREATE A NEW HIGHLIGHT REEL THAT'S FILLED WITH YOUR ACCOMPLISHMENTS! YOUR SUCCESS IS YOUR RESPONSIBILITY! HAVE A WONDERFUL DAY!
#MelanatedGENIUS®

10/8/16
We often reflect on the past and say where WE should be in our lives, relationships, and careers; but the truth of the matter is, WE'RE where we're supposed to be based on the CHOICES & DECISIONS WE'VE

made. (Some good, some bad, and some make you say what the .... was I thinking about?) Simply put, if WE desire OUR lives, relationships, and careers to be better, WE must consciously make CHOICES & DECISIONS that will bring that reality into fruition, and most importantly, BE WILLING TO PUT IN THE NECESSARY WORK TO ACHIEVE OUR GOALS. No one's exempt from this reality. #MelanatedGENIUS®

10/8/16
Do yourself a favor and find you some HAPPINESS!! However, start with being HAPPY with your EXTRAORDINARY self first, because if you don't feel it inwardly, it's gonna be hard to mask your personal discontentment outwardly. Simply put, EVERYBODY deserves to be HAPPY! Happy!! Happy!! Joy!! Joy!! Get You Some!

10/11/16
Sometimes WE have to step back and allow situations to play themselves out before WE intervene, simply because interrupting the process could impede us from seeing what WE need to SEE, and getting the lessons WE need to get from that situation. Observation is essential to learning. Now put this JEWEL in your CROWN and let your LIGHT SHINE! #MelanatedGENIUS®

2/24/17
SOMETIMES BEING TOLD "NO" ONLY MEANS WE NEED TO EXPLORE (N)EW (O)PTIONS TO ACCOMPLISH OUR GOALS.

9/27/17
When the GREAT GOD of the universe set divine forces in motion on our behalf, WE should expect a change in our circumstances without doubting what WE ask for will manifest. Simply put, when WE ask for a change in our circumstances, WE must also be willing to do what's necessary to change our circumstances. Sometimes WE have to change our habits, environment, and people that can't see our vision, or WE know are toxic to our success. The WORK has to be done.

Have a WONDERFUL DAY! ##MelanatedGENIUS™

10/13/17
WE should NEVER get to the point where WE feel like NO one wants to see US become SUCCESSFUL or accomplish OUR goals, because when WE do, WE take on this ME/US against the WORLD mentality. And trust me, as long as we're on this planet, WE'RE ALWAYS gonna need some assistance of some kind. Simply put, WE never know who will be a BLESSING to US.

Have a WONDERFUL DAY. #MelanatedGENIUS

LIFE don't give REFUNDS, so use your TiME wisely and learn how to ENJOY each moment.

10/5/18
Having a conversation with my husband Alex Clark about the word so, sow, and sew.

1. So in the context of so what? Its so easy to say so what, when life get hard or when faced with a challenge.
2. Sow in the context of what kind of seeds are you sowing in the ground or in other peoples lives.
3. Sew in the context of what are you mending? What are you putting together that will last? When you have the needle of decision in your hand, be careful not to stick yourself.

Analyze and think about where you are today. Hopefully your so what attitude will be changed into sowing a seed and sewing to mend negative situation into a positive one.

Have A Wonderful Day!

10/24/18
Sometimes we NEED to SEE what others have to endure in its rawest, ugliest form, in order for us to count our BLESSINGS. Simply put,

things aren't always as bad as we make them out to be. If nothing else, PLEASE remember this, there's someone who would love to have the BLESSINGS WE TAKE FOR GRANTED. If you haven't counted your BLESSINGS, I suggest you do so expeditiously! Now put that JEWEL in your CROWN and HAVE A WONDERFUL DAY! #MelanatedGENIUS™ #ALSsucks #MySupportTeamIsSTRONG

4/24/19
Sometimes being ALONE is the best thing that can happen to us. Because it gives us a chance to see what were really made of. In the world but not of it.

5/10/19
WHEN WE VALUE OUR RELATIONSHIPS, WE FIND MORE WAYS TO ADD "MORE" VALUE TO THOSE RELATIONSHIPS.

5/16/19
NO ONE IS EXEMPT FROM THE LESSONS WERE SUPPOSED TO LEARN ON THE JOUREY CALLED LIFE; EVEN IF THEY KILL US. SIMPLY PUT, LIFE WILL REWARD OR PUNISH US BASED ON HOW WE APPLY THOSE LESSONS.

5/20/19
When a person is at War with themselves, everyone becomes an adversary/target, even the ones trying to help them. Simply put, we can be our own worst enemy and choose to live in denial.

5/22/19
Once we've seen the TRUTH, we can't UN-SEE it. No matter how hard we try! Simply put, once the LIE has been exposed, its up to us if we continue to BELIEVE the LIE.

5/23/19

When we've reached a point in our lives where were ABSOLUTELY OKAY without everyone liking what we do, what we stand for, and accept the fact that we will lose a few people along the way, that's a sign of true growth.

5/29/19

Whatever we give our POWER (Energy, Attention, Resources, etc.) to, will EMPOWER us, overpower us, or leave is Powerless. Simply put, we must be extremely mindful of who and what we give our POWER to, because everyone and everything doesn't deserve it.

5/31/19

When we understand the science of energy, frequency, and vibration, we become more conscious of our thoughts, what we visualize, and ultimately, how we interact with others and the universe.

Facebook Family!

The JEWEL of the day is:
You have to be your BIGGEST FAN, because you never know when others will stop cheering for you or find another team. You have to be prepared for everything, because the same ones that love you today could be the ones that find a way to hate you tomorrow. ©
#WinnersFindWaysToWin

MELANATED GENIUS
AND
MELANATED BEAUTY CHRONICLES

THE LOOK IN HIS EYES

The look in his eyes told a story that only my heart could feel. The look in his eyes told a story about a journey that God chose for his purpose only. The look in his eyes told a story about the limits man placed on his life; but God removed them. The look in his eyes told a story about work still undone. The look in his eyes told a story about God's Grace, Mercy and Peace.

The look in his eyes told the story about a warrior who was tired of spending holidays, birthdays and special occasions in the hospital. The look in his eyes told the story of a warrior who was tired of fighting asphyxiation, pneumonia and of having collapsed lungs. The look in his eyes told the story of a warrior who was tired of seeing the hurt in the eyes of his loved ones who were devastated by his illness.

The look in his eyes told the story of a warrior who was tired of having nurses in and out of our home. Nurses not showing up. Nurses not providing quality care and not understanding how to care for a man on a ventilator, with a tracheotomy and battling ALS.

The look in his eyes told the story of a warrior who was tired of saying "I'm sorry" to his wife every time he woke her up in the middle of the night. Apologizing for not having care when she had meetings or needed to run errands. Apologizing when she had to lift him on her own, when his legs were too weak to stand, so she could dress him or clean him after he used the bathroom.

The look in his eyes told the story of a warrior who was tired of apologizing for his life when he was willing to die fighting.

The look in his eyes told the story of a warrior who was thankful for the sacrifices his wife made for him to have a good quality of life. The last look in his eyes lovingly told me "Thank You."

In Honor of Alex Clark

Once you have learned to love,
you have learned to live.

Husband,

In honor of your brilliance, your strength and your fight, here's to love, the gift we opened everyday.

You were my balance, my prayer partner, my best friend, my SYMPATHETIC SOUL. I may never experience love like this again and I'm ok with that because the love we shared was not ordinary. We both found our why, we both lived a purpose driven life with a shared vision and mission for our marriage.

I will most definitely miss your smile which brightened up my darkest days. Your beautiful eyes which sparkled so bright. Your heart which allowed me to be loved unconditionally without limits or boundaries and the way your serenaded me both in and out of key. The quality time that you set aside daily just for me. That brilliant mind of yours that took me all around the world without leaving the room.

Thank you for always referencing me as your "Queen" and for treating me like one. Thank you and for pushing me into places that were far beyond my comfort zone. My hearts desires and dreams came true because of you. Rest Peacefully Mr. Wonderful. My life will never be the same.

Love Always,

Mrs. Wonderful

www.ingramcontent.com/pod-product-compliance
Lightning Source LLC
LaVergne TN
LVHW092050060526
838201LV00047B/1330